THE TALIBAN AND I

First published in Bengali as *Taliban Afghan O Ami* in 2013 by Patra Bharati

Published in English as *The Taliban and I* in 2023 by Eka, an imprint of Westland Books, a division of Nasadiya Technologies Private Limited

No. 269/2B, First Floor, 'Irai Arul', Vimalraj Street, Nethaji Nagar, Alapakkam Main Road, Maduravoyal, Chennai 600095

Westland, the Westland logo, Eka and the Eka logo are the trademarks of Nasadiya Technologies Private Limited, or its affiliates.

Original Copyright © Patra Bharati, 2013, 2023
Translation Copyright © Arunava Sinha, 2023

Sushmita Bandyopadhyay asserts the moral right to be identified as the author of this work.

ISBN: 9789357769730

10 9 8 7 6 5 4 3 2 1

The views and opinions expressed in this work are the author's own and the facts are as reported by her, and the publisher is in no way liable for the same.

All rights reserved

Typeset by Jojy Philip, New Delhi 110 015

Printed at Thomson Press (India) Ltd.

No part of this book may be reproduced, or stored in a retrieval system, or transmitted in any form or by any means, electronic, mechanical, photocopying, recording, or otherwise, without express written permission of the publisher.

Translator's Note

In September 2013, the body of a woman was found in the Paktika province of Afghanistan, riddled with twenty bullets. She was identified as Sushmita Bandyopadhyay, forty-nine, from Kolkata in India. The story in the area was that she was killed by Taliban militants, although the organisation formally denied being involved. Subsequently, the police arrested two men suspected of killing her, both of them members of the Haqqani militant network. The murder marked the tragic and violent end of a story that began in the second half of the 1980s in the city of Kolkata, when she met, fell in love with, and finally married, in 1988, a man named Jaanbaz Khan.

Jaanbaz was an itinerant door-to-door salesman from Afghanistan, one of many from that country who have over the 20th Century been known as Kabuliwallahs in India. He belonged to the archetype made famous by the great Bengali poet, writer, philosopher and educationist Rabindranath Tagore in his famous short story *Kabuliwallah*. Sushmita and Jaanbaz married in secret, since her conservative

Hindu parents were completely opposed to the idea of her marrying a Muslim. When they tried to engineer a divorce, she and her husband escaped to his home in Afghanistan, in 1989. This was where her encounters with the horrors described in this book began.

The Taliban and I is Sushmita's extraordinary first-person account of her life in Afghanistan during the time of the Taliban. But that is not all it is. The author links her personal history from the time before she met Jaanbaz Khan to the oppression she found herself facing from her husband's family and other men in Afghanistan, besides the Taliban militants who ruthlessly clamped down on the freedom of women in particular.

Soon after Jaanbaz took his wife to Afghanistan, he returned to India to carry on with his business, leaving Sushmita behind in a country being overrun by the Taliban. Caught in the grips of a violent political movement as well as a violent patriarchy, she lurched from one threat to another to her very existence. At one point, the Taliban sentenced her to death and she resigned herself to being shot before there was a miraculous last-minute reprieve.

In this book, Sushmita brings together multiple threads, among them the barbaric ways of Taliban militants as they begin to seize control of Afghanistan, the incredible level of domestic violence faced by women in the patriarchal family structure and society of that country, the constant threat of war and death in a hostile region with inhospitable climate,

Translator's Note

and the imposition of cherry-picked tenets of Islam to deny women agency and independence. And she does this with brutally graphic descriptions of scenes in which she, as well as other women from both Afghanistan and India, are at the receiving end.

The Taliban and I details these encounters with clarity and economy, evoking horrifying situations that are beyond the imagination of most of us who live in other parts of the world and other social systems. Interspersed with these accounts are analyses and reflections on the traditions, practices, religious teachings and male behaviour that make such atrocities possible.

Reading this book, it is almost impossible to believe that Sushmita survived to write it. Tragically, her escape proved short-lived. With her husband already in Kolkata, she settled down to life in the city with him. But in 2013, for reasons that will never be known, both of them decided to go back to Afghanistan, which by this time had seen the partial retreat of the Taliban and the advent of a semblance of democracy. Those who knew Sushmita speculated that she may have gone back to fetch Jaanbaz Khan's brother's daughter, whom she had adopted during her earlier sojourn in Afghanistan. Others said it was to study the condition of women after the political changes in the country. Yet others believed she had gone there to gather material for a novel she meant to write.

During her earlier stay in Afghanistan, Sushmita—who was called Syeda Kamal or Saheb Kamal by her husband's relatives and neighbours—used to administer medicines to ailing women, particularly those who needed help during childbirth. She was not a trained doctor, but had taught herself rudimentary evidence-based medicine from books in order to help women in distress, for they refused to be examined by the handful of male doctors who were available. During her second visit, when she purportedly returned to Afghanistan to fetch her adopted daughter Tinni, she was appointed as an assistant at a healthcare centre, a job where her responsibilities included filming women who came for treatment.

This book is an explosive and incisive account of the extraordinary experiences of an unusual woman who ultimately became the victim of the very atrocities she has documented. A decade after her murder, as the tyranny of the Taliban plays out again in Afghanistan, Sushmita Bandyopadhyay's book brutally forces us to confront our own complicity in injustice.

1

Salaam to you, salaam. It's the 7th of August 1995. I've been impossibly agitated since last night. I spent a lot of time chatting with Haji sahib and Mamo. Hardly a chat though; they just went on and on about religion. As they say, a little learning is a dangerous thing. That's what has happened to Haji sahib and Mamo. They kept targeting me with their verbal arrows.

Sometimes I answered calmly; at other times I grew furious. But I kept my feelings to myself. I will leave Kabul at dawn tomorrow. There's no question of returning. So I had no wish to hurt Haji and Mamo. I could have easily countered Haji's baseless statements. But why bother? Haji had attacked my country, my religion. He repeatedly said there's nothing in Hinduism, neither good nor bad, but Islam is generous. I wanted to laugh. Generosity? Hah! Can generosity be so dreadful? Can it forcefully hold back an innocent foreign woman? Indulge in physical torture? Issue a death sentence citing the law of the Koran? If this is generosity, what is harshness like?

I am grateful that I could stay for a few days at Haji's house in Kabul. Even more grateful he got me a passport. So I stomached what he had to say. Mamo cooked korma and uriji—their word for rice—for dinner. We ate together.

Haji is pushing fifty but has a maniacal libido. He draws Mamo into a room and locks the door at all odd hours of the day, right in front of my eyes. Shamelessly. He has a total of four wives, but he has officially married only three of them. Mamo is on contract. They live together. So living together is practised in Kabul too? The question has been swirling in my head. I wait after dinner while Mamo makes my bed. The lantern burns dimly.

The city of Kabul no longer has electricity. There was power here when I arrived in 1989. Najibullah's secretary Aslam Khan even had a TV at home. There's nothing here but ruins now.

I turn out the lantern. Haji and Mamo have gone into their room. I fling myself on the bed, but sleep eludes me. How will I sleep? I am about to get freedom after a long wait. Six entire years seem to have been wiped out from my life. Time, which has been unbearably exhausting all this while, will start moving again. The song of the cuckoo in spring will make me wistful once more.

The night is at its darkest now. Silent, desolate. Not a sound to be heard. The dogs bark monstrously from time to time, making my hair stand on end. I stare into the darkness within the room.

Suddenly it occurs to me that I'm feeling frightened at the barking of dogs from the safety of a bed inside a room. But what about the time I was walking over graves in the dead of night, only a fortnight ago? When I passed through the village that was nothing but the home of those who had been killed? When bats flew past me, ripping apart the air with their shrill whines? And the man standing in the cornfield?

I feel a shiver run down my spine. How strange that fear, which could not intimidate me a fortnight ago, is making me tremble now.

So much for living with my husband in our own home.

I wake up very early in the morning and bathe. The flight is scheduled for 11 a.m. Haji lives a long way from the airport, in Mikrorayon 2, in quarters allotted to him when he was a soldier in Najibullah's army. He hasn't given them up.

It's nine a.m. The minutes tick by, taut with tension. The hands on the clock refuse to move. I've been ready since seven in the morning. Mamo has given me tea and roti as usual, but the food refuses to go down my throat. I'm trembling in fear and excitement. How long before I can sit on the plane? It will spread its wings and fly away—and then?

Finally, Haji fetches a taxi for me. All taxis in Kabul are Japanese Toyotas. 'Khuday paawan,' I bid goodbye to

Mamo and get in. The airport is a small one. I present my passport, visa and ticket, get my boarding pass punched and head towards the plane.

I'm climbing up the stairs. Now I'm inside the plane. It's mine! Freedom is mine. I bite my lower lip in relief. Peace at last. I look out of the window. The plane has started moving. Now it races down the runway and flies into the air. First stop Jalalabad, and then Delhi. The plane lands in Jalalabad just ten minutes later. Several passengers get off, and many others get on. I keep sitting. The Jalalabad airport is surrounded by jungles on all sides. Kabul isn't too far away—have the horrors of war, the roars of cannons, the frenzy of the Russians extended here as well? Are the people here also like the ones in Kabul? Has the barbaric Taliban stretched its claws out here too? Has it grabbed power here too?

Many questions crowd my mind. The flight attendant is coming my way with a glass of water on a tray. Perhaps someone has asked for some water. She looks confident. I feel an urge to talk to her, but what do I say? My tongue feels dry suddenly. 'Excuse me,' I tell her.

She hears me, comes closer, and says, her consonants soft rather than hard, 'Yes, how may I help you?'

I feel a little disconcerted. She's a Kabul girl, and she's talking to me in English. But then she wouldn't have got this job without knowing the language. How did she learn, though? Then I remember that schools used to run in

Afghanistan until Najibullah's time ended. The attendant is standing next to me. Now that I have summoned her, I have to say something. So I ask, 'What's the time now?'

'Twelve o' clock.'

She goes away. Her pronunciation isn't perfect. I wonder what to do now, the minutes just don't seem to be passing. Suddenly it occurs to me—how about writing a poem? Something about Kabul. I have a pen, but I need the flight attendant's help. There's no one nearby, however. I look up and press a button. This time, it's a man who turns up. I ask him for a sheet of paper, and he brings me one.

What to write? My pen starts moving on its own:

> Salaam to you, salaam, beautiful Kabul!
> So much humiliation you heaped upon me, dear Kabul.
>
> I have seen battles
> between Rabbani and the Taliban
> witnessed millions of deaths
> heard tales of cruelty
> of homes destroyed
> of men and women slayed in Kabul.
>
> Only strife you may call your own, o wistful Kabul.
>
> And salaam to you too, the United Nations!
> Look upon this land, even though I fear you're blind.
> Look at those who laid down their lives in silence
> People do not hear cries in praise of peace in Kabul.

> Blood flows like rivers today in this land,
> No one proposes to end the war in Kabul.
> Severed heads lie in the snow on the mountains
> Starved bodies despair in the broken homes of Kabul.
>
> And now, as I leave,
> I write in blood over my heart
> a chronicle of your losses, dear Kabul.
>
> Farewell to you, farewell, beautiful Kabul!

Is this poetry? I don't know, but I read it a couple of times. I feel like reading it out to someone at once. But who will listen to it in this land of the ignorant? There isn't a hint of literature or art in any corner of Afghanistan. No, it's not entirely true that there is no literature. And the embroidery here is beautiful—it's the only art remaining here, actually. Even someone who can draw a flower in this country deserves praise, never mind that it's nothing but a doodle.

The plane keeps flying. I am leaving. My relationship with Afghanistan is being severed. I will no longer have to endure the inhuman torture of the Taliban.

I was quite happy until the Taliban entered Afghanistan. Gradually, I had to conform to their diktats. I came here in 1989, and Jaanbaz left in 1990, so despite my reluctance, I have had to cater to many of their demands.

The Taliban and I

Even if you scour every village in this country, you won't find a single boy who goes to school. Thinking of their future alarms me.

In the darkness of night in my bed, I would go back to Kolkata. I would ask my parents, my grandmother, my family: Do you remember me? Do you think of me? Do you think of my favourite food when you eat? I stayed awake late into the night, shedding silent tears. There was nobody here to value those tears.

Women no longer ask for anything here. After years of deprivation, they cannot even imagine getting anything they want. The only right women have is to their husbands' bed at night. They are maids the rest of the time. Any man who considers his wife his priority gets a bad name. Still, marriages are held, children are born, and the population keeps growing.

It isn't as though women seek the company of other men because they don't have freedom at home. But there's adultery within every family, which is, perhaps, not a surprising turn of affairs. A married woman named Khomar lives seven or eight houses away. She has three daughters and ten sons. Nadira, the youngest, got married recently. Her husband had to go off to Saudi Arabia in search of a living. Nadira was disconsolate, having only just tasted the pleasures of being held in her husband's arms. How could she be happy without him? But there was no choice. Her husband's brother was in Saudi Arabia, with a valid visa for a year. As one brother's visa expired, another one got a visa and replaced him. Sex is the only entertainment in this country, so life becomes intolerable without a partner for sex. Still, Nadira's husband had to go, and she spent six months in sadness, tears and isolation.

Then suddenly we heard that Khomar's daughter Nadira was pregnant. But who was the father? Nadira didn't want to reveal the name at first, but on interrogation, she said it was her father-in-law's younger brother. My face contorted in disgust when I heard that. The company of a man in bed can certainly be a matter of pleasure for a woman—but one's father-in-law's younger brother? A man responsible for a sexual encounter that brings nothing but shame to a woman should be stabbed with a dagger. Those who cannot think of women as anything but objects of enjoyment should have their eyes gouged out.

2

November 1993. Time, unbroken, lurches forward at its own slow pace. For all I know, it will go on this way till eternity. I sit in a corner of the veranda, wondering wistfully whether I'll ever go back. The Indian women here no longer dream of returning home.

Kakoli and Shoma have accepted their fate; why can't I? And then I ask myself, why should I? If I accept this, what are my education and my culture worth? I'm not a woman to take such things lying down. Islam doesn't seem to empower women to talk back. They have to accept all kinds of oppression. Or else the men will either divorce them or kill them.

It's only November and yet it has already begun to snow lightly from time to time. One more winter has arrived. I see no effort from Jaanbaz's side to take me away from here. Winter only means sitting quietly in a corner of the room. There's very little sun, which seems to have been driven out by the cold to some other part of the world. Winter acquires a devastating form here. But we have no shortage of food to speak of. Meat, potatoes, onions and Dalda to cook in have been stored in advance to last four or five months. Just dip into the stocks and eat. There's no certainty about food the rest of the time though. It's mostly tea and a potato dish. And to add to this uncertainty, there is malaria. And to treat that, quacks!

My heart trembles to hear of doctors. Abu, my husband's uncle's wife, says, 'Did you know there's a new doctor here, Saheb Kamal?'

They're given to consulting doctors here for no rhyme or reason, even when there's no illness. Once Nadir Chacha's wife was unwell. I was absolutely new here then, unaccustomed to the practices in this country ...

Suddenly Nadir Chacha says, 'I'm going to Mamdekhal, Saheb Kamal. Your aunt is going as well; you come along too.'

I have no wish to go because I'm deeply upset. Only last night Asam Chacha's daughter Fauji passed on some secret information to me. Although it's hateful, somewhere in my heart a pain has begun to grow. There's a woman here named Jahanara, whom I can't trust at all. Anyone who can be involved in an illicit relationship with a man from outside the family can also be involved with someone who's part of the family—such as Jaanbaz. There was always a relationship between them. Jahanara used to be in love with Jaanbaz once. Fauji disclosed to me the details of their relationship last night.

Still, I have to accompany Nadir Chacha. It isn't just his wife, Dranai Chacha's wife and children are coming too. A truckful of people are travelling, much in the same way that sheep are transported back home. A large mattress has been laid out near the partition between the back and the driver's cabin. Sitting at the tail end means a jerky ride. I have occupied a corner.

We're passing the Maktab market. Going there is usually an outing for the women here, just like going to New Market in Kolkata. There's no peace in my heart. I requested Jaanbaz to come with us many times, but he refused. He has no work to do, all he does is stay at home or meet his friends at some shop or the other. No Afghan has any work other than war. Still Jaanbaz didn't come with us. A restless heart cannot find comfort anywhere. If this wasn't the case, I would certainly have been delighted at this moment.

We get down when the truck stops near a ziyarat in Mamdekhal. Ziyarat—that's what graveyards are called here in Afghanistan. The Chachis sit down, the children are running about. Suddenly Roshendar tells me in Hindi, 'Come with us, Saheb Kamal. There's a lake over there, full of fish.'

Having lived in India for two years, Roshendar speaks fluent Hindi.

I am surprised. Fish? Here? I accompany her out of curiosity, and the children come along too. They've never seen fish before.

It's nothing but a small pond that Roshendar has been calling a lake. She has no idea about lakes, but then, why would she? The pond does have fish. They look like small carp from back home. Pona maachh, as we call them. There's very little water in the pond, it's barely knee-deep.

'Let's go in and catch fish with our scarves,' I tell Roshendar in Hindi.

She's frightened. 'I'll drown,' she says.

I laugh and go into the water to show her that nobody can drown in such a shallow pond. Still, she doesn't agree. Suddenly Nadir Chacha appears with a heap of pomegranates. I ask him to hold one end of the scarf, and he walks into the water too.

We catch about a dozen fish, but on closer look, I have no desire to eat them. They may look like the fish I'm used to in India, but, in fact, they're not. They're foreign, like me. While we're busy catching them, people suddenly begin to run in every direction. The shops close rapidly. Those who were milling about are now running for their lives. The entire area becomes deserted.

Suddenly a group of belligerent Russian soldiers charge in our direction with their rifles pointing towards us. For a moment, we stand stupefied. Nadir Chacha says, 'We're in trouble. There's a machine in the truck. (They refer to AK47 guns as machines here.) None of us will go back home alive if the Russians see it.'

I begin to sweat at this and jump out of the water.

The truck is parked not ten yards from us. I'm staring at it, terrified. I don't know what to do. Meanwhile, the Russian soldiers have advanced a long way. Where there was a large crowd earlier, not even a dog is to be seen now. Only us. A faint hope rises in my head. I pick up a rock and strike myself hard on the head with it. I can feel a wound opening up on the right-hand side. In unison the Chachis and the children ask in Pushtu, 'Why did you do that to yourself?'

It felt necessary to injure myself mildly to save all of us. Pressing my hand down on the wound, I race towards the truck. The Russian soldiers are nearby now. Swiftly shoving the gun beneath the mattress, I lie down on it and begin to groan. I press down hard on the wound to make more blood flow. It begins streaming down my face. Still, I keep pressing down on it. The soldiers are watching me closely. I am racked by anxiety. The Chachis are standing close by, holding on to their scarves. The slightest mistake will mean giving the game away. The soldiers ask Nadir Chacha in broken English, 'What happen?'

Nadir Chacha stands there as though he has no idea what's going on. I look at the soldiers. Pretending to speak through great pain, I tell them in English, 'I hit my head against the door and injured it badly. We're here to see the doctor.' Knowing that Russia and India have friendly relations, I add that I'm Indian.

The soldiers don't ask any more questions. They only say, 'Don't just keep waiting here, go meet the doctor.'

There's no more reason to worry now, there's no fear of being killed. We don't dare stay there anymore. Nadir Chacha asks everyone to climb into the truck and starts driving.

Everyone marvels at my presence of mind and courage. Not that we visit a doctor. I pass several days in unbearable pain but don't dare go to the doctor.

'Madam, Ma ... dam!'

Jolted out of my reverie, I turn back from the window and find a flight attendant offering me a box of food. I'm taken aback at first, but then I'm myself again and reach out for the box.

Six years of indescribable experiences cruelly displace my beautiful moment, a stable reality, taking me back repeatedly to my days of captivity. My courage and my refusal to accept servility forced me to take this difficult decision—a decision that put a death sentence down as my eventual fate.

I realised I had to escape. I could not stay trapped within the vortex of Islam if I was to gain release from this country and find freedom. I would have to break out of the vortex. I would have to defeat a force way stronger than me. I would have to oppose the fraud being perpetrated under the guise of religion. The Taliban took advantage of the hospitality here to push the entire country towards an impenetrable darkness.

The Taliban and I

Why talk of the Taliban alone? Numerous proponents of Islam are opposed to progress, they have demolished it repeatedly. Let's go back to 1927 for example. The writer Syed Muztaba Ali was in Kabul then. In his book *Deshe Bideshe* (*At Home and Abroad*), he wrote that the king at that time, Amanullah Khan, was determined to ensure education for women. His wife Soraiya Tarzi lent him support. So, even back in 1927, some two thousand girls in Kabul used to go to school in their burkhas. Apparently, they even played basketball and volleyball in the high-walled compounds of their schools. Amanullah felt that even if they didn't learn a great deal, it was sufficient that the girls were going out and getting some physical exercise instead of being locked up in harems.

King Amanullah even brought about some changes in clothing. For instance, he banned the 10-metre robe for men and introduced adreshi or western garments in the form of shirts, trousers, coats and hats. Not conforming to this dress code would invite punishment. Women's garments were changed as well, to keep pace with men. Knee-length frocks and dresses, tight long-sleeved blouses, translucent stockings, high-heeled shoes, gloves and hats became their regular clothing. There would just be a fine net veil hanging from the hat. The bolder a woman, the looser her veil. Syed Muztaba Ali revealed another reform that Amanullah had instituted. Which was to tell everyone in Afghanistan not to accept a maulana as their spiritual leader.

His next major reform came in the form of an announcement: I am not in favour of the veil. I am sending women to Turkey without burkhas for higher education. To study medicine. I want freedom for everyone. If a woman wants to go out on Kabul's streets without a veil, I am prepared to help her. But I don't want to force anyone either.

However, soon, the mullahs united against Amanullah and declared him a kafir. They staked a claim to protecting the traditional path of Islam and labelled anyone who supported the king a kafir too.

Some of them told the rest, 'Do you not know Amanullah has sent women from Kabul as gifts to Mustafa Kemal Ataturk of Turkey?'

One of the maulanas gathered courage and spoke up. 'No, they're going to Turkey to study to be doctors.'

The others burst into laughter. 'Women will be doctors! Whoever has heard of women being doctors? You might as well say they're going there to grow moustaches.'

In 1929, the mullahs collectively anointed Bacha-ye Saqao (the water-carrier's son) aka Habibullah Kalakani as king instead of Amanullah. Bacha-ye Saqao used to be the leader of a gang of robbers. So, in one stroke, the people of Kabul apparently became genuine Muslims again. Another announcement followed to the effect that Amanullah was an infidel because he had made everyone study algebra and geography and had said the earth was round. Those mullahs were the Taliban too, were they not?

As for today's Taliban, I have my doubts about their religiosity. They may impose hardcore Islamic practices on others, but how many of them do they follow themselves? Their main objective is to stoke resentment among people. They are taking harsh, mandatory steps to confine the children of the new generation within the bounds of fundamentalism. They are closing down schools and colleges. The Taliban are closing the door to education, because education takes people towards progress, a scientific outlook and away from religious superstitions. Everyone in Afghanistan lives in unbearable circumstances.

My first experience with the Taliban came in 1994. Before this, I had heard everyone say peace would be back in the country and the war would end now that the Taliban were here. Who were these Taliban? Where did they come from? No one knew. Some Afghans call them messengers of Allah. We belong to Islam, they say, and Allah has sent messengers from the heavens to save us.

I saw the Taliban for myself soon afterwards.

3

How long can you bear an overcast sky when there's a wedding ceremony? The dazzling sunlight in the east is a pleasant sight today. Naeem Chacha's son Mahim Khan is getting married. All of us at home are invited, but there's no question of any of us going. Any of us meaning the women. How can a new bride, who's been married only ten years, possibly go to someone else's house, even to attend a wedding? It's all a matter of honour.

Still, whether anyone else goes or not, I will. I'm beyond these yardsticks of honour and prestige, for I'm a Bengali. What social standing can I possibly lay claim to? So I'm going. This is my only spot of brightness within this dark, repressed existence. I don't know whether it's a real moment of joy, or just a farce masquerading as one, but at least I can forget everything for a little while. I have to attend every ceremony, since the burden of my marriage and the responsibilities it brings are only mine to carry—my husband is not here. A relationship that has not taken me to the pinnacle of emotions—though it is supposed to be my most intimate one. What has it actually given me besides low self-esteem, regret and extreme suffering? The many-hued dreams of love and romance have been eaten away, as if by white ants. Still, I cannot ignore my social duties. But it's all so strange, for where neglect and humiliation are a constant, duty is nothing but a joke. With no rights, no foundation. What Jaanbaz had was a violent desire to possess. And what I had was an endless ability to sacrifice my being.

Anyway, I have no time to ponder over any of this. I must bathe at once and get dressed. Naeem Chacha's family will leave for Ghazni at exactly ten in the morning. The bride lives in Ghazni.

I must now go to the same house where I was welcomed after my wedding with four poached eggs cooked in ghee, naan and doogh, a kind of buttermilk. The bride's father is named Rafiq Khan. He's a nephew of Jaanbaz's. Jaanbaz's name is connected with another name for me now. This name is not truly mine. Not my real name, but one that has been imposed on me: Saheb Kamal. I find myself perplexed sometimes. Who am I? Saheb Kamal, or my past self?

Rafiq Khan's youngest daughter, Rehana, is getting married to Mahim Khan. Ghazni is two hours away from our village Sarana. The road runs across three or four mountains. I have my bath with the two buckets of hot water my sister-in-law Gulguti has brought me. Not just bathing, there's nothing you can do here without hot water; you need it for everything. No one dares come into contact with water that isn't heated; it will freeze even the marrow, like solidified coconut oil. I give Tinni a bath too, after completing mine. How can she not have a bath when her mother is having one? She stood at the door of the bathroom all the while I was inside, her teeth chattering in the cold. But no one was able to take her away. How would they? If Ma is taking a bath, she is surely going somewhere. Tinni is terrified I'll go without her, so she doesn't risk letting me out of sight.

It's exactly nine in the morning. Tinni and I are off to Naeem Chacha's house. They live a short distance from us, to the west. I call everyone here Chacha or Chachi. Oddly, no one here uses any form of address for others. Everyone's called by their name, whether it's your father or uncle, mother or aunt, grandfather or grandmother, anyone. But I find it uncivilised to do this. Myagai Chacha has two sons and a daughter. The two sons are called Naeem and Masoom, and their sister's name is Bibisamsa. She's married. They were all young when their mother died, and Myagai Chacha married again. His wife's name is Dangi.

There's no end to Dangi Chachi's sacrifice. In the Mahabharata, Gandhari had blindfolded herself voluntarily because her husband was blind. And Dangi, married into a Pathan family, jumped from a high balcony voluntarily when she was four months pregnant, destroying her foetus and suffering the intense pain that followed—just so that her stepchildren would not develop any resentment, suspicion, anger, hatred or hostility towards her because she had a child of her own. Masoom, Naeem and Bibisamsa are her children now. Can there be any greater sacrifice?

When I reach Naeem Chacha's house, the women are dancing in a circle in the yard. An Afghani dance. Kayim is playing a beat on the local drum. He's the local barber, who is called the 'dom'. And no one but the dom can play the drums here. Anyone else who wants to play them will have to add the word 'dom' to their name as a suffix.

Now the dancers gather around me. Saheb Kamal must dance too, they clamour. What a nuisance! Me and dance? They won't take no for an answer. I don't know the first thing about dancing, but they don't care, Saheb Kamal knows everything there is to know. And so, a dance it is. Not just any old dance, either, but the *khyamta* of the dancing girls from my homeland.

After this, a convoy of vehicles starts moving. The road winds up and down around the mountains. Sunlight sparkles on knee-high snow. Wherever you look, there's nothing but white, without a single touch of colour. The snow is blindingly white. Our vehicles race across the snow, most of them tractors. Russian tractors. The same tractors that carry heavy tools that are used to till the land.

We reach Ghazni when evening is about to fall. We are made to sit in a heated room. While we get busy chatting, some of the unmarried girls who have come to attend the wedding dance on the veranda despite the cold. Some of them are singing:

> *Turur paal mijoyongi posbin makh dana ba na*
> *Guldanada na jaiyam guldanada na ...*

> When my hair blows in my face, I break out in spots
> So I won't go into the garden, no, no, I won't ...

Suddenly we are startled by the roar of guns being fired. We jump to our feet and rush outside, where we see sparks from a hail of bullets. Everyone's running about in confusion, trying to hide wherever they can. Flames from a rocket launcher come into view. A column of fire rises into the sky and disappears. Bullets are flying over the roof of the house. I hear screams all around.

What should I do? I can't make up my mind. I'm standing alone on the deserted veranda. Where's Tinni? I call her by her name. As I'm about to enter the room in the right-hand corner, someone says, '*Chiro je?* Where are you going? *Odarieja.* Stop. *Bia guli wakam.* Or I'll fire.'

I no longer have the strength to move. I can see about a dozen men scaling the high wall and dropping to the ground one after the other. I'm trembling with fear. Some of them approach me, and one of the men asks, pointing his machine gun at me, '*Siddique chirda?* Where's Siddique?'

I know Siddique. He is Rafiq Khan's eldest son and the bride's brother. I don't answer the militants. Who are these people? I don't know, but they don't look like Mujahids.

They look like a terrorist group or extremists. Before this, I have never seen such people here; they look just like how terrorists are depicted in films. The same clothes and masked faces, with only the eyes visible. They scare the living daylights out of anyone who spots them.

Getting no response from me, they begin to fire in the air, saying, *'Siddique monde raja, mug der waqt nasta.* Show yourself at once, Siddique, we don't have much time.'

I stare at them woodenly. I cannot quite tell why they're calling for Siddique. What do they want? Now they begin to shout, *'Gor, chir na raazi, mug dakor eomkh dabardar kaam.* We're going to destroy this house and everyone in it if you don't show up.'

Another of them says, *'Khodayke ayom priyadam.* I swear by God, we won't spare a single one of them.'

A little later, they begin ransacking the house. The scene is horrifying. They are running amok, kicking away everything in sight.

No, they cannot be Mujahids. The Mujahideen aren't so uncivilised. They behave in a cultured manner and communicate clearly. They will visit even their greatest enemies at home, ask politely for the head of the family, and request that the person they're looking for be handed over to them. I have seen for myself how, when the Mujahideen behead Christians for not reading the Kalema, they personally escort the wives and children of their victims to a safe place. Who are these people, then? And why, for that matter, are they calling for Siddique? It all seems foggy and mysterious.

I don't know what I should do. There's no doubt that I could be the lamb set up for slaughter. You never know, if they don't find Siddique they may well turn their guns on me instead.

Meanwhile, there's the sound of firing again. Not too far away either—someone standing right next to me is firing in the air. All their attacks are being launched against the sky today. Afghanistan's sky is riddled with bullets, it isn't safe or intact anymore. The blue colour of the sky has vanished entirely.

Two of the militants have opened the main gate. Other militants are streaming in. Four or five of them are breathing down my neck now. One of them tilts his head, looks me up and down, and tells the others, '*Tas tul ugra, da khaja saranga kali agusthal.* Look, everyone, this woman is dressed in a shirt!'

Then they ask me directly, '*Tu aili dagasa panjapi kali agusthal? Sarmiyeze na?* Why are you dressed in shalwar-kameez? Don't you have any shame?'

What should I tell them? Where has everyone in the house gone? Can they not see me being harassed? Am I supposed to shout for Siddique Ahmed? Why are they all hiding, why aren't they coming together as a group to take on these men? I'm sweating profusely despite the bone-chilling cold. My eyes are filled with tears. I rack my brains, but I cannot fathom how to deal with this situation.

One of them asks again, '*Tu na wai Siddique chiroda?* So you won't tell us where Siddique is?'

Gathering my courage in my hands, I say, '*Tas oili na maane? Ma nada maloom. Siddique sukda?* Why won't you believe me, I really don't know. Who's Siddique?'

I have no choice but to lie, or they're going to pin me down again. I add, 'We don't live here, we're only here for a wedding.'

Now it becomes clear why they're looking for Siddique. They say, 'We're the Taliban. Tell Siddique to come here. We have a score to settle with him. He's been spreading lies about us.'

Taliban? The same people who conquered Urgun a fortnight ago and are supposed to be holed up here in Ghazni? The same people who say they're willing to lay down their lives to bring peace back to Afghanistan? I am perplexed now.

They continue, 'We're the Taliban, we're the real Muslims. But Siddique is telling everyone we're here out of greed for power. What proof does he have? If he cannot provide evidence, we will shoot him dead. Tell us at once where he is.'

Shoot him dead? They're going to kill Siddique Bhai? When I don't answer, one of them grabs my dupatta. Another man rips my kameez. Then someone kicks me in the back. I fall on my face and start crying in terror.

Suddenly, Siddique's mother and wife come out of the room. Siddique's mother starts crying too and asks the Talibani men, 'What's she done to offend you? She's married to someone from a different family. Why are you beating her up?'

The Taliban pay no attention to her. They go back inside the rooms, pull out everything they can and dump it all in the yard. They empty out sacks of sugar. From clothes to food to quilts and mattresses and pillows, they're taking everything they can and piling them outside. Unable to overturn the huge drum of flour, about ten of them urinate in it. Then they drag all the women out and kick them till they fall on the floor of the veranda. The children are screaming at the top of their voices. Rattling machine guns, wailing infants, shrieking women, roaring militants—all of these sounds reverberate loudly around us.

After this comes the most horrifying incident. They finally locate Siddique and drag him out to the veranda, where they begin to beat him up mercilessly. Siddique's mother races inside and comes back with a copy of the Koran Sharif. 'By this Koran Sharif, I plead with you to let my son go. He's made a mistake. Kill him if he says anything about you ever again.'

Bursting into laughter, one of the Taliban men snatches the Koran from her and hurls it into the middle of the yard. All the women and Siddique mutter unanimously,

'*Bismillah, Bismillah Rahmaner Rahim, La Ilaha Illela Muhammuddin Rasul Allah.*'

Do the whispered pleas of these devout Muslims reach Allah? Do the Taliban have even an iota of humanity? They're supposed to have come from Pakistan to bring peace back to Afghanistan. Are they really heralds of peace? They even use the white flag as their symbol. What an extraordinary way to use the traditional flag of peace!

Even more extraordinary is to see those who declare themselves 'the only true Muslims' fling the Koran Sharif to the ground. Are these really the people who will bring peace back to Afghanistan?

The Taliban militants don't seem satisfied with all the destruction they have caused so far. They ransack the house again before leaving and take all the money and jewellery they can find, leaving behind only anguish and misery. Until an hour ago everyone was in a joyous mood. Now they're holding their heads in their hands. Siddique is groaning in pain. His wife Ameda has laid down their baby and is gazing at his stricken face. I'm sitting with Tinni in a corner of the room. My clothes are no longer intact. I've barely managed to cover myself with the dupatta the Taliban had grabbed. I'm on the verge of tears again. Are these the in-laws I deserved? Is this the marital home I had dreamt of as a young girl? A place where my clothes would be torn to shreds by fanatics? Back then I had no idea I would be faced with such a situation.

Back then. Back when I would sneak off to New Market in Calcutta to meet Jaanbaz. He was so in love with me, and it wasn't as though I wasn't in love with him. His clear desire, though not expressed explicitly, attracted me. I was enticed by all the things he said without seemingly saying anything. One day he said, 'Come with me for a movie, Mita?' That was what he used to call me before we got married. I said, 'What movie? An English film?'

'English film? Listen, Mita, decent women don't watch English films.'

'What are you talking about, Jaanbaz?'

'What I'm saying is right. I watched an English film once, it was dirty.'

I realised what kind of film he might have picked. One day he showed up with two movie tickets. Probably for a film at Metro, I don't remember clearly. I don't remember the name of the film either. It had Tina Munim, Smita Patil and Rakesh Roshan in it. When I was crying at the end for the character played by Smita Patil, Jaanbaz said, 'What are you crying for? It's only a film. Nothing like this happens in real life.'

I told him, 'If this were to happen in my own life, I would kill both my husband and the other woman. I don't want a husband who would betray his own wife. I'd prefer to be a widow.'

How strange that I am not a widow today. The nature of the betrayal may have been different, but it was a betrayal nevertheless.

We retrieve the quilts and mattresses from the yard. No one can sleep without them in winter, and sleep will not excuse us because of what we have been through. But there is no question of food.

It is seven in the morning. Time to go home. Breakfast has been sent by Siddique's in-laws. Nearly half of Ghazni's residents are Parsis, who are referred to here as Parsibans. Siddique's wife is a Parsiban. Parsibans are modern compared to Pathans. Their ways of living, their attire, their style of conversation, are all different from those of Pathans. They're posh, you can say.

We set off with the new bride. No one is singing, but there are no flashes of machine-gun firing either. We are travelling in silence. Morning turns to afternoon. It isn't snowing today, but the sky is overcast. Like light, intermittent rain, the occasional snowflake drifts to earth.

The road ahead is shrouded in fog. Our vehicles have their headlights turned on. This has been my first encounter with the Taliban, the first time I have seen them.

I run inside as soon as we reach home. Where I encounter another unexpected situation. Gulguti is sitting in my room, her face battered and swollen. She is staring blankly at me. My heart twists in pain on seeing her. I ask her, 'What's happened?'

She says, 'Shaowali beat me.'

'Beat you? Why? And why did you let him? Why couldn't you break his arm?'

'He punched me on my nose and in my face and back because it was taking me some time to make the naan.'

Blood is still trickling out of Gulguti's nose. Shaowali couldn't care less—he's sitting in his own room, singing at the top of his voice. I walk in. Stopping, he says, 'What's this, Saheb Kamal, when did you come back?'

Sternly I say, 'It's none of your business when I came back. Why did you beat Gulguti?'

Shaowali says emphatically, 'I do as I please. I'll beat her again if I want to. Who are you to ask?'

His impudence makes the blood rush to my head. I cannot hold myself back. Rushing to the cheshkhana, the winter kitchen, where the wood for the fire is stored, I pick up a chopped log and return to Shaowali's room.

Guessing my intentions, he pounces on me like a tiger. I tumble to the floor, but I jump to my feet immediately and aim a blow at his head with the log. It falls on his shoulder instead. Screaming in pain, he drops to the floor. Now it's my turn to beat him with the log, which I do to my heart's content.

Suddenly someone delivers a kick on my back. Turning around, I see it's Kala Khan. Grabbing my hair, he begins to rain blows on me. I don't get the chance to retaliate.

I return to my own room, devastated. There are no tears in my eyes, only flames. A smiling photograph of Jaanbaz is hanging on the wall. I pull it off the peg and smash it to the ground outside the house. What else has he given me besides humiliation?

I'm forced to pay the price for an invisible right being exercised on me. My dream has turned into a nightmare. Love has wrapped itself around me like an incurable disease. I want freedom, but how will I attain it? Who will give it to me? Merely leaving this place won't amount to freedom. If I can stay here and teach all the women to protest, I will consider that freedom. But do I have it in me to do it?

Queen Laxmibai went to war against the British in men's clothing. Then why can't I fight against these thickheaded Pathans? Laxmi Swaminathan led Subhas Chandra Bose's Jhansi regiment. Why can't I lead the women here into a revolution?

Nawab Wajid Ali Shah's mother, Begum Auliyah, ignored the superstition against crossing the seas and risked her life as a Muslim woman to meet Queen Victoria in order to save her son's kingdom. Why should I, as an Indian woman, lag behind?

I don't consider men and women different, except in biological terms. If a man can take on the appearance of a wild beast instead of hiding his face in shame when persecuting a woman, why can't a woman turn into an ogre too? The clash of male and female egos is a natural outcome of the barbaric oppression and atrocities perpetrated by men against women over centuries. It's women who have been fractured both physically and mentally. Men use women as they please, while remaining completely indifferent to their true worth.

I have seen a painting by a French artist titled 'Liberty Leading the People'. The artist used his imagination to draw liberty as a woman leading hundreds of armed men to war. If the flag in her hand is the banner of victory, her uncovered breasts symbolise motherhood. It is the natural propensity of women to draw everyone to themselves—they are in fact vessels of strength, and yet it is they who are insulted and humiliated.

It is to avenge this humiliation that women have to rise in armed protest. When men humiliate women continuously in order to meet their physical needs and establish their authority, it becomes essential to awaken the spirit of the women's movement.

I will arouse it too. I will create a new kind of revolution in every home in Afghanistan. Afghan women must be made to realise that they have their own identity. They must understand that they have the power to protest.

I know it won't be easy. The women here are frightened. Never mind protesting, they dare not even leave their homes alone. But I must convince them that I am here for them: Just follow me. Do as I do. Learn to say the things that I say. Draw men to yourself with your love, make their lives worthwhile, but retaliate when they hit you. Do not forgive male tyranny under any circumstances. A man's love is a valuable asset for a woman, but justice can't be traded for it. They point to the Koran Sharif, claiming it allows a man to have four wives. They lie. The Koran doesn't say a man should marry four times without reason. You must protest. Oppose your husbands' second marriages. Say no to a man sleeping with two wives in the same room.

I can barely get out of bed. My entire body is ringing in pain. My lips are impossibly swollen. I have become used to being beaten up by my brother-in-law. But despite the pain, I feel a sense of peace. Yesterday I managed to land several blows on Shaowali.

4

'Wake up, Saheb Kamal, wake up.' Shaken awake, I shoot up in my bed. Covered from head to toe in blankets, I haven't even realised that it's morning already. I go outside, where my three brothers-in-law are clearing the snow. Another day has begun in Afghanistan. The same tedious life, devoid of any variety. Still, I go on, as I must. I eat to survive. I have conversations with others to pass the time.

It's been three full years in Afghanistan. Jaanbaz has gone back to India with Asam Chacha. Our days were passing pleasantly in love and in lovers' quarrels, in excitement and in placidity. For Jaanbaz's sake I endured all the pain and suffering I was subjected to. But I couldn't enjoy his company for very long. Waiting up for him one evening, I fell asleep without meaning to, and woke up suddenly at midnight. A lantern was burning in the room. There had been times when Jaanbaz hadn't come home all night, but I hadn't felt quite so anxious on those occasions. After being out all night, he would appear in the morning with a broad smile on his face to seek my pardon. Though he wouldn't explain why he had been out all night.

But that night, I began to feel restless. His not being home was making me nervous. Asam Chacha was not home either. He had said goodbye to both his wives and others the previous day and left for India. Twenty-four hours later, Jaanbaz had still not returned. This didn't feel right. He hadn't been his usual self in bed the night before. It hadn't occurred to me all day, which wasn't unusual. Many things, real and unreal, which take place between husband and wife in the darkness of their bedroom or in the privacy of their bed, are not remembered during the busy day afterwards. But now I recalled that his lovemaking was more intense, not like on other days. As though he was going far away from me, or as though we would never be together again. Now it felt as though there was a suppressed sadness in his behaviour. But what could the cause of this pain be? Had he left me here and gone back to India? But how was that possible? He loved me, after all, I was his wife. No matter whom he keeps his secrets from, a man will always confide in his wife. No, Jaanbaz couldn't possibly do anything so inhuman. He loved me more than life itself. Had a Mujahid killed him by mistake? The lantern was burning dimly. There was a strange play of light in the room. I made a mental note to give Jaanbaz a piece of my mind when he came home the next day, so that he would swear off spending nights outside the home without informing me. What kind of reckless behaviour was this, not coming home at night? I tossed and turned in rage.

There was no sign of Jaanbaz even at noon the next day. I couldn't concentrate on examining my patients. He was never so late. Just the other day, he had spent the night at his aunt's place without telling me, but he had come home at dawn. Everything was probably fine, but still my heart was trembling with an unknown fear. I had a persistent feeling that Jaanbaz had gone somewhere far away and that he couldn't hear me calling out to him.

The atmosphere at home seemed strange too. I noticed a defiance in everyone. Everyone except Gulguti. Her eyes were red, as though she had cried a lot. Of course, she wept over her fate regularly. My brothers-in-law did not seem as calm as they usually were on other days; on the contrary, they appeared belligerent. Sadgi didn't normally stretch her legs out on the veranda. Today she was doing just that as she drank tea with raisins and talked loudly with her husband, Kala Khan. Which was impossible when Jaanbaz was home, for none of his brothers would sit chatting with their wives in his presence.

It was one in the afternoon. I was sitting on a pillar outside the front door, scanning the road anxiously. Suddenly I saw both of Asam Chacha's wives, Abu and Serina Chachi (Adraman's sister) coming towards our house. My heart leapt into my mouth. It was over, it was all over. He was gone, Jaanbaz was gone. Not all my screams would bring him back. Jumping to my feet, I began hitting the wall with my head and broke down in tears. They would probably bring his body into the yard soon. It was all over. I went up to Abu like a mad woman and wrapped my arms around her. Everyone put their hands on my head. Still sobbing, I said, 'Who's done this? Who? I won't spare whoever it is. I will kill his entire family, no one will survive.' Asam Chacha's first wife, Pablu Chachi, said, 'I'd like to see what you can do.' Enraged, I punched her in the face. She collapsed on the floor, whimpering.

Abu grabbed me and forced me to sit down on the ground. 'What's all this? Why are you hitting her? Your husband left by choice.'

I didn't know how much time had passed. I tottered to my room. I had stopped crying a long time ago—I was no longer in mourning. However, something seemed to have come to an end. Darkness appeared to have defeated daylight and was spreading across the earth. A dry desert wind was blowing noisily. The cows were mooing constantly near the draw-well. The hens were strutting about with their wings aflutter. A cock began to chase a hen, whereupon another one puffed up its crest and forced the pursuer to move away. I sat at the window, gazing outside blankly. I seemed to have forgotten how to blink. I didn't feel like sitting there anymore. Covering myself from head to toe with my scarf, I lay down. Those who had come by left after offering consolation and advice. I realised it was not death or the Mujahids' bullets. He had run away. He was alive. Therefore, I was bound to meet him one day. Lies, all lies! Love is a lie, all promises are lies. I was fine the way I was before he came along; I had vowed not to fall for another man. Why did I have to marry then? And if I did, why not someone from my own country? Someone spoke up from within me, 'You yourself are responsible for this.'

'No, it's Ruma who's to blame,' I tried to justify my choice to myself.

My heart shot back, 'Do you really think it's Ruma's fault?'

– Of course. She's the one who introduced me to Jaanbaz.

– Liar. Ruma may have introduced you, she didn't ask you to marry him.

– Actually, I saw a real man in Jaanbaz. And so, I fell in love with him.

– Then why blame Ruma now? And is this your real man? Don't you remember Sourav? Couldn't you have rejected Jaanbaz? But you didn't make the slightest effort. Die now!

―――

Jaanbaz has left. My memories of him are fading. I haven't forgotten him entirely, but the love I had is covered in layers of hatred now. There are no tempestuous currents of love in my heart anymore, only waves of resentment that crash on the sand in exhaustion.

Can this be real? Because what has happened to me is anything but real. Three years have passed since Jaanbaz left for India. He spent only two years and seven months with me, sweeping me up in happiness and love in that brief period of time. Now, all I get are cassettes with his voice recorded on them, once every two or three months. In them, he says I can join him once the war stops.

I had neither the time nor the inclination to get to know Jaanbaz properly before our marriage. We met perhaps once a month, at a fixed time, between three and four. At Flury's restaurant in New Market. The time it took to drink a cup of coffee or eat a pastry was all we had to get to know each other. How well could he have gotten to know me either? But I realise the utter futility of asking these questions now.

Will I really be able to pull the curtain down on all relationships? I get out of bed and sit in a corner of the veranda. The afternoon is coming to an end, and an erratic breeze has sprung up. The incessant cawing of crows has died down, but one particular crow is creating a cacophony. The rain has let up today after two days of continuous downpours. But there's no sign of Mr Sun. He's probably exhausted still. I feel wistful on such cloudy days. The starving heart wants something, wants to hold someone close, wants to melt at a loving touch. I have quelled my demanding heart every time. Poor heart, it doesn't know there's no water to be had in an arid desert. Why do you seek affection, sympathy and kindness? Does the person you want it from even understand what your eyes say?

As a couple, we couldn't be more different from each other. Jaanbaz likes Pushtu music, I prefer the songs of Tagore. There's a frenzy of music when he's home. He prefers to talk of love in a coarse language, while I seek feelings from the heart. For him, even roughness is a fortune to give away. For me, a beautiful, refined sensation is a bounty if I get it.

The wilful heart refuses to accept the realities of place and time. Wanting, giving, speaking with glances—all of these tender things have been lost somewhere. When the sun sinks in the west, its vermilion glow paints the entire sky red. And then darkness fills the earth. Jaanbaz's love is exactly like this.

My body feels hot, my breath is like fire, my eyes are red. I'm exhausted. I've had a high fever for three straight days now, along with a splitting headache. I've been lying alone in the room, no one has sat down next to me to soothe my brow with a cooling touch. No one has asked if I feel poorly. I'm thirsty. For love. I have concealed tears in my heart. Jaanbaz had tried to fill my life with some moments of pleasure, but is that possible now? I had never imagined that the love between Jaanbaz and I would turn directionless and erect a barrier between us. All-conquering love has become all-devouring today. I had left for Afghanistan with love as my companion. Afghanistan and America were the same to me at the time, since I hadn't been to either of the two countries. The need to understand how they are different from each other hadn't arisen until then. I hadn't read Afghan history either. Still, I travelled to a foreign land in 1989, having fallen in love with and trusted a foreigner. And how much respect had this trusted foreigner accorded me? I came here as a guest for a mere four to six months. But the village of Sarana trapped and choked the guest. Here the days were filled with nothing but horror. Not a day passed without at least ten to twenty people being killed. Not a night passed without bombing and firing. From 1989 to 1990, I witnessed the war raging between the Russia-Najibullah combination and the Mujahids.

After 1990, the civil war began. Something the Afghan population wasn't remotely prepared for. Everyone had imagined that the war would end with Najibullah's departure. In 1990, the Mujahids signed a pact with Russia and Najibullah, according to which the Russians would leave for their own country and Najibullah for Delhi. So Russia was trying to deliver a final blow before calling it quits. I still remember that day, which came shortly after Jaanbaz left, as though it's unfolding in front of me right now …

Gulguti and I had just taken a sip of our tea when the ground shook as though an earthquake had struck. We were silenced by the grotesque sound of a missile. I had been suffering from malaria for quite some time. The fever had subsided, but a constant intake of quinine had left me weak. Everyone scattered at the sound of the missile. Confused by the volley of their footsteps, I ran too, despite the weakness in my body. I was no longer concerned about my health. I went to the roof first. The houses here are earthen, but they all have ceilings; they're not thatched with straw like the huts back home. The roofs are made of earth too. Every year before the rains, they make a thick mixture of earth and dusted straw and layer the roofs with it. There are stairs leading to the roofs, which turn dangerous when it rains or snows.

I climbed up to the roof to see where the missile had fallen. I stood at the eastern corner, from where one could see clearly in every direction. I saw everyone fleeing eastwards along the road on the southern side. Among the crowd was Daulat Khan. He had come twice with Jaanbaz to meet me at my parents' home in Calcutta when we weren't married; he had had tea in my family home. I raced back downstairs to the front door. Daulat Khan, Qadir and others were running past the house. All of them were members of the same party. I ask Daulat Khan, 'Where has the missile fallen?'

Still running, he answered, 'Port Kalake. On the houses up there.'

Our houses were located lower on the slope. I was stunned. This meant that Golbibi's house had been struck down. Golbibi was Gulguti's younger sister. I started running with the rest of them. My head was spinning; there was a film of darkness in front of my eyes. Still, I ran, pushing aside the branches of the trees laden with red fruits, and then darted across the wheat fields. It was almost impossible to run through the knee-high snow. I strode forward as though I was marching. Someone was calling out my name behind me: 'Saheb Kamal!'

I had no time to stop for her. One more family had been destroyed. The call came again, and I realised who it was: it was Abu. She knew I had been laid low by a fever for the past three days, and going out in the cold would mean a relapse. But I didn't care.

The entire responsibility for the people here seemed to have come to rest on my shoulders. An unseen obligation had taken hold of me; I could not push it away even if I tried. I wasn't going to submit to class or religion or caste; I would not hesitate to lay down my life in the course of supporting the helpless. I would certainly not ignore the collective problem for the sake of my personal ones. Standing by the powerless in their times of trouble was my sole duty.

Even from a distance, I could already hear the sobs and lamentation. The house had been reduced to rubble; no one would believe there was ever a building there. But this wasn't Golbibi's home; it belonged to a mason.

Everyone got busy clearing the rubble and extracting bodies. A large slab of earth was removed to reveal a woman with a little girl in her arms, still holding a piece of naan. Both had been crushed. Tears were streaming from my eyes. Everyone was home when the missile hit; none of the occupants survived. The invasion-happy Russians were dealing out death blows before leaving, with Najibullah's support. There was just one cry that could be heard clearly in the air: 'We will stay in power, even at the cost of the blood of people.'

So much blood! My head began to spin again, I saw stars; I no longer had the strength to stand. I was trying to call out to someone, I could not stay on my feet any longer. My eyes were closing. My neck could not hold my head up. It slumped. *Can anyone hear me? Any of you? I …*

I don't know how long I remained in a stupor. When I recovered, I found myself lying in bed, with Gulguti and Abu by my side. Abu stopped me from sitting up. She's my father-in-law's younger brother's wife. Her heart is full of love for everyone. It was Abu who had welcomed me into the family with sugar and dry fruits on the day I arrived as a new bride from Calcutta. She is Dranai Chacha's sister, his only sister. Dranai Chacha's mother's name is Mushoki. Everyone calls her Mushoki Adi. So do I.

Mushoki Adi's family lives in Shelgar, which is right next to Ghazni. She has had a strange life. Her husband is missing and his whereabouts are still a mystery. He left when

Abu was five. Abu's brothers Dranai Khan and Nadir Khan were also young at the time. The disappearance should have been investigated. Unfortunately, people couldn't care less. Mushoki Adi brought up her three children all on her own.

Abu was married to her cousin Begai Khan, my father-in-law's brother. She became a widow very young. She was a beautiful woman, but didn't marry again. Everyone in Afghanistan is related to one another in some way. There's always a family connection, no matter how distant. Everyone in an uncle's neighbourhood is a chacha, everyone in an aunt's neighbourhood is a *dostan*. In-laws are referred to as dostans here.

Abu loves me like her own daughter. As she strokes my brow, I'm reminded of my own mother. I'm her only daughter, the apple of her eye. Perhaps she waits impatiently for me every day. *When will Sumi be back? When will Sumi put her arms around me?* My heart is restless, Ma, my eyes yearn for you. I don't know when I will come back to you. My obstinacy and foolhardiness, my determination to keep my word and a small mistake, have torn me away from normal life, Ma. I have been snatched from your arms and brought face to face with a very cruel reality. I am bereft today. Forgive me, Ma. Forget me. Tell yourself you never had a daughter. You can do it, can't you?

War has been declared in every city, every village. Najibullah keeps saying he'll leave but is still here.

5

The year is 1990. Desperate to oust Najibullah, the Mujahidin are now waging war against him. Millions of corpses lie on the roads, covered in blood. Who's going to oppose this cursed war? Only the intervention of all the nations together can stop this war. But where are they? I try to explain to everyone in the village that we need unity. If we aren't united, if we remain greedy for power, this war will never end. The Mujahids have an office at the far end of our village, about two miles from our house. Which means our lives are at risk as well. If a missile is aimed at the Mujahids' office, we'll be destroyed as well. Missiles don't always land on their precise target. The terrible war between the Russians and the Mujahids could lay waste to all of Afghanistan.

Many people have left their homes and set off for Pakistan, uprooting themselves to journey towards the unknown. Nearly half the village has been emptied out. Trucks piled with people leave daily. Tractors and other vehicles ferry villagers to safety. But my father-in-law's brother Azam Khan isn't willing to leave. His view: If I have to die, it will be in my own country; I won't go to someone else's. All the windows of the house are bricked up so that bullets cannot fly in. There's an underground room equipped with essentials for us to use for the duration of the war. All the women know something is about to happen, but no one knows what it is. Everyone who stays back inevitably joins the Mujahids. Their meetings go on all night. The Mujahids patrol the streets as soon as darkness falls. Robbery is rampant. It's become dangerous to go out at night.

One day I hear screams and climb to the roof. Peering through a hole, I see about fifty people beating up a man. Later I learn he is a spy who has been passing on information about the Mujahids to the Russians.

Food has become scarce in the country. Everything has become prohibitively expensive. The common people cannot afford to buy food. The population starves while the Mujahids live in luxury.

Snow is falling in a drizzle, the sky above is grey. Where are the lifeless Afghan people headed in this bone-chilling cold? Towards which watershed moment? With what hope? Najibullah is showing no signs of surrendering—or that's what the Mujahids say—though my view is different. Terrorised Afghans get death warrants from the Russians. War! Either we will be victorious, or we will destroy everything. The Mujahids call on everyone, 'Arise, people. This is no time to sleep. Najibullah is selling our country, our motherland, to the Russians. Save the country! Reinstate the sovereignty of Islam!'

Afghans become anxious at this. They gather together to raise cries of '*Naara-e-taqbeer, Allah-hu-akbar*': We will follow our destiny, we are with the Mujahids, we will go to war, we will lay down our lives, but we will not surrender our country.

Pleased, the Mujahids respond, 'We're happy today. Our hearts are full.'

The people say, 'No, don't let your hearts be full just yet. The road is long.'

And then the war spreads across the country—a horrifying war. We begin to pass our days in terror. Fifty of us live in the same underground room. The darkness is impenetrable, but we dare not light a lamp, lest the Russians fire missiles at us. Sometimes I go out of the room under cover of the night, gaze at the sky, and fill my lungs with fresh oxygen. Then I go up to the roof to look at the city. Fires burn everywhere. The roar of cannons and gunshots is all there is. There are the screams of people and the smell of gunpowder. Ghastly. Gruesome.

I sit down with my eyes closed and stick my fingers in my ears. Then I run back to the room inside which fifty people are stuffed. Everyone with an underground room in their house has taken refuge there. A trial by fire. From 1989 to 1995. Beginning with Najibullah and the Russians

The Taliban and I

in power, and ending with the fundamentalist Taliban in charge.

At first, the opposition of the Mujahids to Najibullah seemed natural. A strange change in popular opinion, an erosion of democracy. To understand the Afghan revolution, it is crucial to remember that the economy of Afghanistan and the everyday lives of its people collapsed not in 1989, but much earlier. The corruption-ridden Mujahids could not be trusted to eradicate these problems. It was as though the Afghans deliberately chose the path of destruction.

Even as people across the world today are set on a path of progress, Afghanistan is getting dragged deeper and deeper into a primitive darkness. At a time when everyone in the world seeks education, the majority of Afghans don't know how to read or write. The country is passing through an unbearable crisis. In my view, Russia and Najib had a constructive vision initially and were not intent on a destructive revolution. Had the Najib government remained in power, there would at least have been schools and colleges and factories.

Najib's party used to be controlled by those who were liberal and somewhat educated. Their most important task was to spread education, and to pay attention to the everyday needs of society. But the Mujahids did not support these goals. They knew only too well that supporting Najib would mean burying their leadership ambitions forever. So they had no qualms about spilling the blood of millions in order to defeat Najib.

The Taliban have succeeded the Mujahids. Their objective is to preserve their self-interest, demolish the new age and bring back the dark times. They had to lay down their lives while providing support to the Najib government and were expelled from the country. Their houses were destroyed. The Mujahids put their entire strength into ensuring there was no democratic solution involving the people. The Najib government was unstable then, caught between constructive reforms on one side and the onslaught of hardcore fundamentalists on the other. Najib was bewildered. How was he to make progress in the face of such powerful opposition from the Mujahids?

---

20 November 1990. The confidence of the Russians has begun to wane. The icy winter of Kabul is almost upon us. Everyone in the village says winter is our constant companion, like family. Even in the emptiness of the cold, planes fly overhead, and there are rocket attacks too. Defenceless people call on Allah. The war is ready to swallow the people whole. Personally, I wish for a victory for Najib. No matter how violent the Russians are, at least Afghan citizens will be rescued from inevitable anarchy. Law and order will be restored.

But the rural people will not accept Najib. The Mujahids have convinced them that Najib is a debauched man and a drunkard—an enemy of the nation. Uneducated folk don't subscribe to the logic of analysis.

And yet, even the one night I spent in Kabul has convinced me how advanced the Najib government's programme is. Despite the war, there is order.

The war has been resumed since November. The days are getting shorter. The sky is overcast. Winter winds are blowing. There are light showers of snow, which turns into slush on the streets after melting. There are occasional gusts of icy wind. The fog doesn't clear before nine in the morning. The entire country is shrouded in darkness at night. You can't even see the person standing next to you in the street. Lanterns flicker in every home. Kerosene oil is both expensive and difficult to get. Thefts and robberies are rising in the cities. Armed Mujahids are on patrol everywhere. Food is scarce. Cows have stopped giving milk because there is no fodder. Children are crying of hunger. It is time for apples and grapes to ripen, but most families have no money to buy them.

The Mujahids are determined to topple the Najib government. Rows of tanks move towards Kabul. Everyone passes their days in terror. Hundreds and thousands are forced to leave their homes and join the war. The sparks fly all over Afghanistan. A beleaguered government is forced to accept defeat. There's nothing more to be done.

The Mujahids come to power. But this does not lead to peace, for everyone launches themselves on the currents of factional conflict. Every moment is like the sullen silence of the night. People are busy preparing to counter the enemy. Rivers of blood flow in Kabul. The famine has spread from the cities to the villages. Everyone is fatigued. They have lost interest in both the Mujahids and Najib.

Finally, the war drums die down. The Mujahids are overcome with joy at having snatched power. But, unfortunately, the war does not end. By now all the partiality for one side or the other has drained out of people. They have realised that this peace is not permanent. They know the cessation of bloodshed is not in their fates.

The Taliban enter in 1993 using the civil war as their weapon. First, there were the fundamentalist Mujahids; now we are plagued by the fanatical Taliban. Blunted by history, the people of Afghanistan surrender their past and present without resistance to Allah's so-called messengers.

I gaze helplessly at the plight of the Afghans. What kind of land is this where there is no such thing as security, where no one cares about the law, where there is neither order nor freedom. Everyone has to obey the Taliban; they have to do as the Taliban say. The Taliban are the jailer and the people, prisoners. Rebellion takes shape in my head. It is necessary to establish a feminine movement, and immediately. No one feels they have any right to assume power of any kind. It isn't easy to rouse a town full of dead people. How much can one hope for victory when the mental, physical, economic capabilities of the common man have dwindled? Still, I march forwards. Calmly and with quite a bit of self-confidence, I try to make everyone understand that the Taliban are wild and violent, and that they are misusing religion.

6

It is 1994, possibly the month of September. Mornings arrive after sleepless nights spent worrying. One day I fall asleep at dawn and wake up quite late. I go out at once. It's a damp, cold day. No one in the country smiles anymore. The women are housebound, the men are perturbed and the children are terrified. The sky no longer conveys the greetings of a new light when the darkness of the night passes.

Madalam Chacha's wife has been having a terrible stomach ache for some time. She's all but stopped eating. Chacha's daughter Raisa comes to take me to her mother. I am astonished at what I see—her abdomen is impossibly enlarged. There can be several reasons for it, one of which might be ovarian cysts. Can an illness be diagnosed on the basis of assumption? Especially by someone like me, who believes in evidence-based treatment?

I tell Chacha, 'Take her to Pakistan at once for treatment. Or else it will be difficult to save her.' The Taliban come in the way. Women going to doctors? How's that possible?

After all, women are animals or the root of evil conspiracies, or objects of some kind. Madalam Chacha doesn't take his wife to Pakistan, and she lives for only two more months. This is how women are condemned to die here.

The Taliban has persecuted me unremittingly. I had escaped to Pakistan earlier but was caught. Then I escaped again a month later. Kakoli came to see me before my second escape, and seeing her reminded me of how a man often sleeps with two wives in the same bed. My body recoiled in revulsion. How twisted their conjugal life is. The thought disturbs me constantly. Thinking of the woman who is forced to become the second victim of the night makes me rebel. This is unbearable humiliation for a woman.

I have repeatedly invited danger upon myself in trying to gain plaudits. Because people at home like my cooking, my brothers-in-law often invite guests and force me to cook for them, beating me up if I refuse.

Torturing women is an act of great valour for any man in this society. I have no space in my husband's house for a moment's quiet reflection. No woman in Afghanistan has any space to think or analyse. Eat, chat, and go into your rooms with lanterns as soon as it's dark. Battle against poverty and unemployment. Fight the stifling shadow of traditions and fundamentalism and ignorance and lack of education. How will seeds of new ideas sprout here? How will anyone learn to think differently?

Privacy is one of the greatest gifts of modern civilisation, but no home in Afghanistan offers it. This suffocating life stands in the same place every day, refusing to move on.

There's no privacy, but there's loneliness. Ironic, isn't it? In six years, the Kabul evenings have not once brought me a spring breeze. It has never felt romantic here. Only insufferable. Especially from December to February, when it snows every evening. There's darkness everywhere—not a song in anyone's heart, not a word of love in anyone's head. All I want is to go back to my room in Kolkata and sing along with Tagore's songs or read Nazrul's or Jibanananda Das's poetry.

Had they been born in Afghanistan, would Kazi Nazrul or Jibanananda Das have become poets? For all you know, they wouldn't even have been capable of writing a letter. As men, all they would scream is, 'Bring me food. Wash the clothes. Light the lamp. Give birth. Clean the snow. Submit your body at night.'

Initially, the sex life in Afghanistan appeared repulsive to me; it made me nauseous. But after six years, even that has become attractive. There is probably some sort of perversion in the relationship between women and men in this country, or so it seems to me. But in this perversion lies everyone's pleasure, perhaps their only form of entertainment. Life here is nothing but war and arid deserts. Maybe sexual perversion is the only oasis. I try to remain indifferent to the harshness of sex here, I try to preserve the faith and the values, the likes and dislikes, of my Bengali self. And this has been possible only because of Jaanbaz.

Sometimes I wonder—the extreme torture the Taliban submitted me to, the way they beat me till I was half-dead, even tearing off my clothes—was it all because I offer primary medical treatment to people? Does the desire to punish me stem from my sowing the seeds of rebellion among people? Is there no other provocation? I feel there are other reasons. To the Taliban, I am a kafir. A Hindu, someone from another religion. A Bengali. A woman. And the Koran has repeatedly warned against marrying a kafir.

I escape a few days after being persecuted to inhuman lengths by the Taliban. The first time, they capture me in Pakistan and lock me up in a room. My brothers-in-law stand guard round the clock. When I escape a second time, I run all night, through graveyards and across ditches, and am about to get on a train at dawn when the Taliban capture me again. Then there is a trial, and I am sentenced to death.

The Koran stipulates death for women like me. I am falsely accused of being an adulteress. Because I had the audacity to defy their authority and escape twice.

It is 22 July 1995. I was captured two days ago. Even my second attempt to escape did not secure my freedom. The trial took place at my husband's nephew Rafiq's house. Fifteen members of the Taliban and several of my husband's uncles were present. After day-long discussions on the 21st, the judgement was delivered. I was to be shot dead. Jaanbaz's uncles made many requests, they pleaded with the Taliban to wait until Jaanbaz returned.

The Taliban did not entertain them. They said: 'We cannot allow our nation to come to harm because of a kafir. This will bring our women a bad name. The whole world will point its finger at us accusingly. They will say we have insulted Islam, and we have insulted the Koran, which clearly says that when a woman is wayward, try at first to restrain her. But if she refuses to be disciplined, kill her. Else it will be a sin. And those who accept this waywardness are sinners and will go to hell. Therefore, she must die, or we will be guilty of flouting the holy tenets of Islam.'

So it has been decided that I will be shot at twelve seconds past forty-five minutes past eleven on the morning of 22 July. Apparently, it is an ideal time for the execution of a death penalty. Last night, preparations were made for my last meal. Rafiq's wife and daughters-in-law were crying for me. The Taliban and my in-laws were downstairs in the guest room. Dranai Chacha, Mamai Chacha, Abdullah, Bismillah—they were all present. After dinner, Siddique told me that no one in the family ate properly.

It's nearly two in the morning. A moonbeam falls on the wall clock. Its hands seem to be radium-lit. Rafiq's wife is lying next to me, fast asleep. I am awake. I think of Jaanbaz. He will never see me again. Perhaps he will marry again after some time has passed. Will he remember me when he is with his new wife? Won't he blame himself for my death? Will he be able to lead a normal life after this? Why did he abandon me? I cannot fathom the reason. He married me, brought me here, and then went away—why?

Perhaps Jaanbaz has a hand in this death sentence. Perhaps he has asked for me to be killed by the Taliban. Why didn't he make arrangements to pick me up from Pakistan? Why didn't he talk to me even after my phone call?

I wake up from my last sleep at first light. I didn't eat at night, and I feel no urge for tea now. Everything will be over in a few hours. My heart weeps when I think of my grandmother and my parents. Ma! Baba! Forgive me. I am being punished for my disobedience to you. I wish I could see you once again, Ma.

The night will turn into day again. Life won't come to a halt. The sun will rise, the stars will twinkle around the moon. There will be snow, there will be searing heat too. Everyone will remain, everything will remain. Only I will not. Death is approaching me, one step at a time.

It is exactly nine in the morning. I am sitting in a corner, waiting for the final moments. Death is no longer approaching me one step at a time. It is now right in front of me. It will release me from this material world very shortly. I have no one of my own here.

It is 9.37. The sun is bright and warm. Several women come up to me and say, 'Come with us, we will bathe you. The Taliban say you are an impure kafir. They will convert you to Islam after your bath. You will go to heaven then. When a kafir dies a Muslim, they are purged of all sin. Allah sends them to paradise directly. And those who convert you go to heaven too. Jibreel will not interrogate you. Allah will pardon you for your sins.'

They are talking to me in Pushtu. I accompany them without demur. After the bath, they sprinkle rosewater on me and then empty a bottle of perfume on my shoulders. Then they take a length of white cloth, just like a bedsheet, make a hole in the middle, and slip it over my head. They say, 'Haj pilgrims dress this way. You're converting to Islam, so you don't have to go for Haj. But you will get the merit one earns when they perform the rites of Haj.'

It is exactly 10.27 now. I am taken to the guest room, where fifteen members of the Taliban are sitting in a row, reading the Koran. I am their lamb to the slaughter today. They read verses from the Koran while I sit in front of them. Someone says, 'Read the Sura Fatiha.' Waiting for the appointed hour of my execution, they begin reading out loud, starting with Allah-hu-Akbar. Apparently, this will prove beneficial for me. Perhaps I will float directly upwards to paradise after being shot.

The Taliban and I

We must appreciate the greatness of the whole act. Of seeking benevolence and benefits for someone about to be killed by their own hands. This is like the common joke around here—thank heavens she died of a bullet wound in the head; at least her eyes have been spared.

I seem to have been turned into a robot. My entire body is numb. I stare blankly at the Taliban. One of them asks, 'Any message for your husband?'

'Tell him I'm the happiest person on earth today,' I say.

Dranai Chacha is part of the Taliban, or so I think. After all, they were sitting in his house the other day with a map, asking him for the best route to India and whether they could keep themselves abreast of news from Afghanistan if they stationed themselves in Delhi, Mumbai, Calcutta or Amritsar. Why were the Taliban asking him this?

Dranai Chacha did cleverly manage to avoid answering them. But I remember trembling with fear. Since then, I have told myself over and over again: 'I could have warned my fellow countrymen if only I could reach India somehow.' But all I have done is suffer here in agony. I haven't found the road back home.

How isolated I am in this moment; there is no one here I can share my pain with. I have realised how fearful the approaching footsteps of death can make a person. I'm afraid. I'm terribly afraid. I want to scream, 'Don't kill me, don't kill me!'

Eventually, I groan, 'Let me go, please. I will never run away again. I will do whatever you tell me to do. I won't ask for food if you make me starve. I won't ask for water if you don't give me any to drink. Just let me live. Don't kill me till my husband returns.'

But no, the Taliban pay no attention to my entreaties. They keep reading the Koran. My dulled eyes roam around the room. There are several pictures on the wall with verses from the Koran on them. A clock too.

Suddenly my eyes stop. What should I do? I will have to leave the world in just thirty-two minutes. All my dreams, all my hopes, will leave with me. I will not even see my mother in my final moments. She will weep all her life for her daughter.

If only I could go home in my final hours. I would have no regrets if they were to kill me in my own homeland. They could humiliate me, make my life even more unbearable, and still, I wouldn't complain.

I bid farewell to you from a faraway, alien land, my India. My final respects are for you alone. May I be born again in your arms. Having said goodbye to my country, I turn towards the Taliban.

The thing hanging on the wall that my eyes had stopped at gives me an idea. This opportunity won't come again.

The object in question is an AK-47.

I learnt how to fire an AK-47 from Jaanbaz. I had fired several times in the air during Kala Khan's wedding. My temples are throbbing. I can tell that my face is contorted with rage, hatred and vengefulness. Throwing caution to the winds, I grab the gun from the wall and point it at the Taliban.

'What do you think of yourselves?' I let fly at them. 'You think you can cast a slur on anyone you like and shoot them? I won't give you the chance. I will not die at your hands. I will kill all of you first and then kill myself.'

They realise this is not an empty threat. Dranai Chacha tells me, 'Calm down, Saheb Kamal. I am here, I won't let you come to any harm.'

'Calm down?' I roar. 'Have you heard what these people have said about me? That I'm immoral. Explain to me what's so immoral about me.'

One of them jumps to his feet. His eyes are fixed on me as though he will finish me off any moment now. It's a fearsome look, but today I am not afraid. I am determined to kill before I am killed—I will not accept defeat. I will leave a mark on Afghanistan.

'How dare you, you fallen woman? You demand justification? You ran away not once but twice. What is this but immorality?'

'I did as I pleased, and I'll do it ten times again if I have to. As for daring, I'll show you today what daring is. Don't you look me in the eye, I don't live at your mercy—I'm from India.'

Another man from the group forces this man to sit down. All of them are unarmed, and I am standing with my back to the wall, holding the gun in a way that will let me fire at any of them. I release the safety catch. Pressing the trigger now will mean a volley of sixty shots. None of them has the courage to stand up now. Dranai Chacha says, 'Calm down. What do you want? We will do it.'

'Listen to me carefully. I have informed the leader of my country that if anything happens to me here, all the Afghans in India should be killed. So I suggest you make arrangements to send me back. Or you will be responsible for your countrymen's deaths.'

One of them says, 'Why should so many Pathans have to die because of a single woman? Send her back home.'

'But how dare she threaten us with a gun? We won't let her go without teaching her a lesson. We will whip her at least twenty-five times.'

The blood rushes to my head.

'Do you think I'm your father's property? Let me see which of you dares do it. Go home and whip your mothers and sisters first!'

The Taliban finally give in. 'Very well, then. Go back to India.'

7

Gulguti has no past nor future. What can anyone's life be like when her husband is alive and yet is not with her? She even has to take care of Musa's wife. Everyone here knows that Gulguti has an illicit relationship with Musa. Everyone except Musa's wife. But if Gulguti has been labelled as being immoral, why doesn't Musa have the same reputation?

I wish I could tell Musa's wife, 'Don't even entertain the possibility that your husband is faithful to you. He tasted blood long before he married you.' My whole being seethes in loathing when I see Musa romancing his wife. How dare he live a happy married life after sending someone hurtling to destruction and turning their whole life into a failure? But there's nothing I can do. I have only one handicap: this is not my country. I am completely alone here. If I inform Musa's wife, he will shoot me dead.

There's no such thing as law and order in this country. Anarchy is the only constant in Afghanistan. You can kill anyone you want without repercussions. There's no police, no police station, no minister or elected representative. People do as they please. Four or five people die every day in Moktab at the hands of quacks from Arabia. These so-called doctors operate on their patients without anaesthetics. The same quack treats ulcers as well as cancer. I doubt if there's another country in the world so mired in despair. They don't even have a post office here.

Gulguti's life makes me very sad. Where will she end up? Who will look after her? All her dreams have turned into nightmares. Once, though, those dreams were a reality. The things she wanted and the things she got mattered. Gulguti's parents had got her married to Akbar Khan with great hope. That was such a long time ago—Gulguti was nineteen then, and Akbar, sixteen.

Marriages like these, where the grooms are younger than the bride, are not uncommon here. After my sister-in-law Sultanbibi's uncle died, his widow married her husband's younger brother. Her daughter and her new husband were the same age.

In Gulguti's case, too, age was not a hindrance. Your husband is your god, even if he's younger. Gulguti would wash his feet when he came back home after playing. Akbar's grandmother was still alive then; he used to sleep in her bed. He would tell everyone if Gulguti asked him to sleep with her instead. He had no idea of conjugal relations. Even when his grandmother cajoled him to sleep in Gulguti's bed, he would return to her, claiming his wife had pulled away the quilt in her sleep.

Akbar grew up playing this game of hide and seek. Then one day, he paid several visits to Gulguti's room, starting in the afternoon. Gulguti wasn't a child, she knew what was going on. She would only throw arch looks at him and smile. Suddenly Akbar lost his temper and asked her, 'What are you laughing at? Why can't you tell my grandmother that I will sleep with you?'

Gulguti said, 'No, I won't. I asked many times before, but you didn't bother. You can tell her yourself now.'

Akbar was furious. He grabbed Gulguti and bit her on the lip before leaving the room. Gulguti felt spring invade her heart at the height of the rainy season. She heard a sweet melody; waves of romance rose within her. The rain seemed to have stopped; the wind stilled. Gulguti remained where she was, overwhelmed. Akbar would come to her tonight, she thought. He would soothe her, he would arouse her, he would bring peace to her. And so, suffering the pang of separation, she waited. She never bared her heart to anyone—she didn't have the language for it. Wistful and silent, she felt her heart thump in her chest. Gulguti looked out of the window. Where had such madness sprung from on this quiet afternoon?

Even if no one else had noticed what Akbar was up to, Adam's wife, Dangi, had. Without wasting any time, she informed the elders. Then she got busy dressing Gulguti up for her first night with her husband. All the women gathered to sing:

> My husband is coming to my room tonight
> My life is coming to me.
> My husband is coming to my room tonight
> My mother-in-law has three sons
> One is the green mole on my neck
> Two are necklaces.
> My husband is coming to my room tonight
> I won't let anyone else in.
> It will be only him and I.
> My husband is coming to my room tonight
> My dearest, my lover, where are you?
> Why do you delay so?
> Come at once, come to me ...

It was 9 at night. Dangi told everyone, 'Come on, let's fetch Akbar.'

Dangi went off, followed by the others. Akbar was surrounded by his younger brothers, all of whom told him, 'Go on, don't waste time here.' Naksira Chachi tugged at Akbar's arm. Although she was his aunt, she was young enough to banter with her nephews and nieces. Akbar feigned reluctance once or twice but did not protest too much. They pushed him into the room and barred it from the outside. Then they ran to the window to eavesdrop. Gulguti knew they would do this; she had done it too in Dangi's case.

So when Akbar came up to her, she whispered, 'Sit quietly for a while. Everyone's at the window.'

Akbar sat down in a corner. But his eyes were on Gulguti, who was gazing at the floor.

Akbar couldn't hold back any longer. 'Come here,' he told Gulguti. 'Let them eavesdrop. The curtains are drawn, no one can see anything.'

Gulguti went close to Akbar and surrendered herself to him.

My heart was full on hearing Gulguti's story. Why is the heart so restless, I asked myself. But why not? It's entirely natural. I am a human too. And not only humans, animals too have physical desires. Some can resist them and others cannot. Those who can are enlightened human beings.

I was so engrossed in Gulguti's story that I had forgotten to greet the onset of evening. Guncha's husband had left a pile of carrots yesterday. I was going to cook them with potatoes. Sadgi would cook if I asked her to, but her cooking was hard to eat. So I would have to go to the kitchen, which was some distance from the house. The yard was muddy. I put on the shoes I used when it snowed. I sliced and diced the potatoes and carrots while chatting with Gulguti. There was a low fire burning in the stove. Sadgi had laid out everything I would need, the pans and ladles, all of which I had bought in Pakistan. They were kept in a tin trunk and brought out only when I cooked. The women here didn't know how to use them …

My thoughts grind to an abrupt halt. I have forgotten I'm on a plane. I have spent the entire journey recollecting the past. The aircraft lands with a jerk. Ah, what a relief! I've returned to my country at last.

8

It's almost evening. The sun has dipped on the western horizon. It's been nearly two months since I came home to my country. Everything is as it was or should have been. But my brother—he's gone to a place from where no one returns.

Kallol was born after me. He departed from this world in the July of 1993. Love proved to be his undoing, and he came to the realisation that he had no other option. My mother couldn't take his sudden death; it broke my father's heart too. Everything changed overnight. I wasn't prepared for this. I became silent. All of this had taken place in my absence. This loss was a serious blow to me.

My brother. A relationship that cannot be interchanged with any other bond, not for all the money in the world. I have lost him. Jaanbaz and the rest knew everything, but they didn't inform me. How cruel, how heartless they have been with me. Death is inevitable, today or tomorrow. Surely this inexorable truth cannot be denied. Truth is often bitter. But does that mean it should not be spoken?

I haven't been able to scream my heart out. I haven't shed tears. I haven't collapsed in grief.

Nothing but a pain has remained. An excruciating pain. He's gone. Gone. My heart is like a skeleton from which the defeated, rotting flesh has fallen away.

I found out about Kolu, as we called Kallol, as soon as I arrived home. I was a mental wreck after this. At the same time, I learnt of another tragic event. This isn't the age of Hitler or Mussolini, but even in 1995, with the twenty-first century round the corner, the same gruesome events are repeating themselves.

It is September 1995. I pick up the newspaper on waking up, only to be shocked out of my wits. The Taliban have ruthlessly murdered Najibullah. Not only did they kill him and his brother, they also hung the bodies on light-posts for three days, letting vultures prey on them. People all over the world have condemned this barbaric killing.

After this, the Taliban run amok, capturing Kabul. They begin their rule by jihad and fatwa, persecuting women and confining them to their homes, beating them up on the streets for not wearing burkhas, cutting the men's hair and demolishing TV and radio stations.

Can today's reality bring me back my idyllic childhood? The past cannot return, and yet the unbearable part of my past always hovers over me. Gazing at the festive skies of autumn in Calcutta, I am reminded of the overcast skies in Afghanistan—skies that never bring good news, skies that offer no hope.

Temporary joys never become permanent, but temporary sorrows turn into a burden for life. I have forgotten all the pleasurable moments of thirty years of my life. Those beautiful days are a thing of the past. But I simply cannot separate the suffering of the past six years from my life. Even in moments of joy, it hunts me down.

It was over religion that my conflict with the Taliban began. How horrific that day was, when they came to my house for the first time ...

It's September 1994. I'm having my morning cup of tea. Rahisa, Jalazi, Bagala, Kamara, Golapi, Zarina and Zorgol will be here soon. They are members of my women's squad, and I am their leader. What I say is the unalterable truth for them. I have taught them a slogan—Mujahid zindabad, Taliban murdabad! Long live the Mujahids, down with the Taliban! Arakat neta Rabbani zinda rahe! Long live Rabbani, leader of the Arakats! Taliban neta Abdul Malik qabar mein rahe! Let the Taliban leader Abdul Malik rot in his grave!

But we dare not shout it in public. We are preparing secretly. Nearly two thousand women have joined my squad. We do all our work in secret. I teach them to fire guns. I used to be afraid at the beginning. But after thinking it over, I realised that fear is the same as death. So why fear? Death will come one day, sooner or later.

I'm almost done with my cup of tea when a banging begins on the front door. Gulguti, Sadgi, Sultanbibi and the rest jump out of their skins. Rising to my feet, I shout, 'Who's there? Why are you banging on the door? What do you want?'

'Who's at home? Come out.'

'None of the men are in. What do you want?'

'Is there a doctor here?'

I rush towards the main door. Maybe it's a patient in a precarious condition. Just a couple of weeks ago, there was a woman whose labour pain had begun three days before she was expected to deliver. She showed every sign of being about to give birth, but then the pain suddenly stopped. I gave her a Syntocinon injection. The contractions began again, and the baby was delivered two hours later. Maybe it's a patient in a similar situation. I go up to the main door and find some people standing outside. 'What is it?' I ask.

'Are you the doctor?'

'Yes, what is it?'

'Where's your dispensary? Where do you examine patients?'

I point to a room on the left. About twenty men barge in at once. I say, 'Where are you going? Stop!' I have no

The Taliban and I

trouble realising who they are. I am quite familiar with such uncivilised behaviour.

It's the Taliban. But why are they going towards my chamber? I follow them. They kick the door open and enter. Right before my eyes, they take the medicine bottles and hurl them to the floor. I lose my head in anger and fear. Racing up, I try to examine the bottles. Unable to contain myself, I burst into tears. I start gathering the broken vials. My hands are bleeding, I have cut my feet on the shards. But I don't care. I am being driven to madness at the sight of my creation being demolished. Its ruins lie in front of me. I have nurtured my chamber little by little, as one nurtures a child. Who am I going to turn to? Who will listen? Protect my chamber, Allah, you are all-seeing—save my creation! Standing amidst the destruction, I don't hesitate to call on their god even.

He doesn't listen. Having decimated my chamber, the Taliban issue a command: 'You! Kafir! Recite the Kalema. Say the words, La ilaha Illallah …'

I grow strong. My tears have stopped. How dare they call me an infidel? I say, 'I won't. I won't recite the Kalema. Why should I? Did the Kalema protect my clinic from you rogues?'

'You won't? How dare you?' They begin to punch me, slap me, kick me.

'Say it! Will you recite the Kalema or not? Say the words, Bismillahir Rahmanir Raheem … La ilaha Illallah Muhammad Rasul Allah …'

'I won't, I'll never say it. I refuse to utter the words you want me to. I am not a parrot. You claim to be priests. Show me where in the Koran it says it is right to beat and force women to recite the Kalema. You call yourselves true Muslims? *You* are the kafir!'

'You dare call us kafirs. We will kill you today!'

They grab me by my hair and drag me across the ground. Two or three of them keep kicking me in the back. The agony! Why don't you make the sky collapse on their heads, Allah?

No such thing happens. The sky doesn't fall. And there's no question of their stopping. They drag me out of the house and dump me on the street quite some distance away. There are crowds everywhere. The roofs are packed. The women are watching from their terraces. All the villagers have gathered. But none of them protests. They don't have the power to protest even if they want to, for the Taliban won't leave anyone alive if they do. They can do nothing but watch in silence.

After a while, one of them stops beating me up and tells one of the others, 'Go get a burkha.'

He runs off at once. Another man says, 'Listen to me, kafir. You cannot go out of the house anymore. You have to wear a burkha. We will kill you if you don't listen to us. You cannot run your dispensary here.'

Suddenly there's a roar like thunder. Someone is approaching us, shouting. Everyone turns towards him and cries in unison, 'Dranai! *Dranai gol ragalai*. Dranai is here.'

Dranai Chacha sprints up to the Taliban and screams with bloodshot eyes, 'You think you have the right to torture my daughter-in-law? Am I dead? I'm going to Pakistan at once to talk to your leader.'

Turning to the crowd, he bellows, 'Aren't you ashamed of yourselves? All you can do is stand and watch? Couldn't you break their arms? Are you men or women?'

The Taliban say, 'No need to talk like this, Dranai.'

Dranai Chacha says, 'Why shouldn't I? Don't you know she's the daughter of a top military officer? If she sends word back to India, they will set fire to all the Pathans who live there.'

I hear him, the Taliban hear him, everyone hears him. His words work like magic. The Taliban give up and leave. Dranai Chacha comes up to me and helps me rise to my feet. He supports me as we walk back home. Then he puts his hand on my head in a gesture of affection. Gravely but with kindness.

9

The swaying of the branches and leaves seems to convey an unarticulated message—everything changes, something comes, something goes, someone rises, someone falls. A wild, rousing wind enters the room through the window to ruffle my hair. A demonic hand is destroying a beautiful, uncomplicated land of snow—the hand of race and religion. The beginning is distressingly familiar, and the end, unknown. And everyone, from the young to the old, is plunging headlong into this uncertainty. Death is child's play here, and yet a new generation continues to take birth amidst this dance of death. Some of them survive, the rest succumb to neglect.

In trying to understand the mystery of these births, I have realised that it is not so much the joy of creation as jealousy and obstinacy that are at work here. The husband has two wives. Neither should be deprived of his attentions. He has to split the nights between them—two nights with the first wife and two with the second.

Even if all three of them sleep in the same room at first, once both the wives have had several children each, a single room isn't enough. They have to be in separate rooms. This means the husband is now in a tug of war. And he is in dire straits, for which man can get going every single night?

Let's say it's the second wife's turn. For some reason the husband hasn't felt like having sex the past two nights, but perhaps he's keen tonight. But he can't, for he hasn't slept with his first wife. So he now resorts to subterfuge. Still, that provides no respite. He must bathe before sunrise if he has had sex, and his first wife knows his timings and habits. So she waits to see if there's water flowing through the drain at that hour—the tell-tale sign. And sure enough, this will be followed by bickering.

The system persists, and the number of children keeps increasing under the pressure to give equal time in bed to both wives. The newborn have to pay for their mothers' assertion of their rights, for the future holds nothing but darkness for them. A baby facing the same future is on its way in Adam's family. His fourth child. His earlier children also saw their first light at my hands—three sons in a row. Adam's wife is suffering greatly, as she does every time she gives birth. Her blood pressure is high. I'm apprehensive about giving her an injection, but there's no option. I have to induce labour pain and, at the same time, stop her bleeding. Eventually, I am left with no choice but to give her the injection. Why do they want to give birth so many times despite suffering so much? It's a boy this time as well.

The women of Afghanistan have so much love in their hearts, though it cannot be expressed. But that doesn't hold them back. Some of them do have affairs. Jaanbaz used to love a woman. Her name was Margalara. Everyone knew of their love—they were neighbours. The tale of their love was played out in the exchange of glances and their colourful dreams. Unfortunately, harsh reality delivered a whiplash to their relationship. Their dreams were shattered. Love bestows fulfilment upon some and invites ruin upon others.

Just as it did upon Pauline. She was in love with Shovon, who used to live in Simjuri, north of our neighbourhood. Pauline gave her heart to him, but he could not honour her love. Instead, he told her friend Shibani that he was in love with her. Pauline didn't have an inkling. By the time she found out, it was much too late.

She wept her heart out when telling me the story. 'I still remember the day, Sumi. It was Saraswati Puja. He took me to a friend's place, overruled my objections and had his way with me. It was clear from his passion that this wasn't the fullness of love; it was just momentary lust. There was no sincerity in it, no question of exchanging hearts. Only thirst, not acceptance. Real desire, which is contained in a frisson, waits for the right moment—Shovon destroyed it. He left me bleeding in his friend's house that night and ran away.'

I kept looking at Pauline. I couldn't imagine love ending in such a dirty and horrible way.

After this, Pauline entered a new phase of life, trapping a succession of men in a web of infatuation and deriving a strange pleasure out of it. How euphoric she was. One day she told me, 'You know, Sumi, when these greedy men confess their love for me, I feel a peculiar revulsion.'

I said, 'What are you saying, Pauline? Everyone's delighted to be told someone's in love with them. You hate it?'

'Yes, I do. Love that has no fulfilment is not pleasure but pain. I pledge my love to a different person every day.'

'How do you do it, Pauline? How does your heart lie about love?'

Pauline recounted her experiences. All I could do was listen; I had nothing to say.

Margala of Afghanistan did not find fulfilment in love either. The man she loved went off to India. She didn't wait for him, got married and gave birth to children. Everyone told me she used to be my husband's lover. I tried to speak to Margala to understand her heart, but I failed. She had come to Asam Chacha's eldest daughter Fauji's wedding.

The bride suffers greatly at Afghan weddings. Unlike in Bengal, where the bride is adorned in fine clothes and jewellery on the day her husband's family celebrates the marriage, in Afghanistan, the bride sits all day long on a folded mattress, covered from head to toe in a silk scarf, which is slightly larger than the bedcover for a single bed. Every time there's a visitor, she has to rise to her feet. Someone else will lift a corner of the veil to allow the visitor a glimpse of her face. She will be let off only late at night, which is when she can go to the toilet.

This will go on for three days, after which the wedding will be conducted by a maulvi. Both she and the groom will be asked three times whether they agree to be married.

Not that any of this took place in my case. It was all quite bizarre. When my father found out, it was like being struck by a bolt of lightning.

I vividly remember the day Jaanbaz proposed to me. I had said in astonishment, 'Marry you? What do you think you're saying, Jaanbaz? That's impossible. Absolutely impossible.'

'But why? I love you. Why marry someone else?'

'Why don't you understand? I'm a Hindu and you're a Muslim. This marriage can never take place. My father will kill me.'

Jaanbaz looked at me strangely. There was contempt in his eyes. I told him, 'I consider you a friend. Of course I love you. But the way friends love each other.'

His response was succinct. 'I never imagined you'd stoop so low. I knew Bengalis were traitors, but now I've seen it for myself. After three years of going around together, you're saying we're nothing but friends? Will you be able to forget my love, Mita?'

His words rang in my ears all night. I heard the echoes continuously, 'Bengalis ... traitors ... forget my love ...'

I lay in bed, unable to sleep. Was I a traitor? Then what about Sourav? All my dreams had been woven around him. There was a storm raging in my head and heart. It was the beginning of my adult life. All that imagination, all that desire wouldn't let me sleep. But Sourav had demolished my castles in the air; he had smashed my desire into splinters. He had come into my life uninvited and touched my heart. But had his touch contained even a single drop of love? If it had, how could he have told Ronita he loved her and invited her into his bed?

'How deeply do you love me, Sourav?' I had asked him one day.

'I love you like the sea,' he had answered.

The sea had turned into a foetid pond. I had asked Jaanbaz the same question. 'How deep is your love for me, Jaanbaz? Is it like the sea?'

He had answered, 'What's that? What's the sea doing here? The sea is visible, but love cannot be seen, it can only be felt. I love you very much, but it's not something one can talk about casually. The union of two hearts is love.'

Marvellous! I realised the significance of what Jaanbaz was saying.

Why was I allowing myself to be troubled by thoughts of Sourav at this beautiful moment, the Sourav who had hurt me, who had not honoured my love for him?

The man who tiptoed into my life subsequently could have plundered everything from me; he could have left me with nothing. But he didn't. He valued me. What was I to do now? On the one hand, there were my parents and family to think of. On the other, there was Jaanbaz. Whom should I give myself up to? No one at home would agree to such a marriage. Impossible. Having spent the night in this quandary, my head was bursting in agony. I had not yet decided what to do. I had never imagined I would be confronted with such an impossible problem. I was racked by these thoughts when my mother asked, 'What's the matter with you? Why do you look so haggard?'

'Nothing at all,' I lied to her.

'I'm not going to believe that just because you say so. Tell me what it is.'

I didn't know what to tell her. I hadn't come to a decision myself. Still, I said, 'All of you are concerned about my marriage, aren't you? What if I do pick someone to marry?'

'If you've decided, tell me who it is. What does the boy do? Which caste does he belong to?'

I suddenly recalled that whenever my friend Hena came to see me, my mother wouldn't let her beyond the drawing room. And after Hena left, she would sprinkle holy water from the Ganges everywhere. I had asked her one day why she did this. She said, 'It's because of those Muslims that we had to give up our homes after Independence and come away to this place.'

How terrible! Muslims are objects of hatred to Hindus because they had to leave their homes when Bengal was partitioned. My mother would probably have a heart attack if I said I wanted a Muslim as my life partner. When I didn't answer, my mother said, 'Well, who is it? What are you thinking?'

'Ma, will you object if I tell you I want to marry a Muslim?'

'A Muslim? Have you gone mad?' She began to weep.

'Not really,' I said, 'I was just testing you.'

Things were resolved for the moment, but not for long. Soon everyone came to know that I was considering marrying Jaanbaz. A fire began to rage all over the house. My father and uncles tried to persuade me to change my mind. Finally, they resorted to beating me.

This was a blunder. I became even more adamant. I would marry Jaanbaz, come what may. Very early one morning, when everyone was sunk in sleep, I walked out of the house. I wouldn't look back anymore, I had to march forward now. I prepared myself. I knew only too well what was coming. I took Jaanbaz to the marriage registry office on Hazra Road at that early hour. It was right next to Kalika cinema hall. My friend Lipika had married Amal at the same place. Many of us were present then, which was how I knew where the registry office was. I didn't have any of my friends with me, besides Luna, who was Manik's wife.

It was time to submit myself. Jaanbaz and I were married without any pomp or blessings, or chants. No religious ceremonies were conducted, neither Hindu nor Muslim. Two hearts came together outside the perimetres of religion and society. But Jaanbaz's eyes said everything he had to. He took my hand as we were going down the stairs after getting married. This was the first time he had held my hand. My heart was touched by colour. I came to an abrupt halt. Was it possible to be so stirred by the intimate touch of a man? Unruly waves of passion were ready to roar, but the time and place throttled us. We went back to our respective homes as though nothing had happened, as though it was all a dream. Fantasy and reality became one that day. The only union in our marriage was that of our hearts.

And now? I'm alone, there's no one nearby. Even if I scream at the top of my voice, no one I call my own will come to me. My voice is choked with tears. Just one question emerges. Why? Why, Jaanbaz? Was there any need for this? Who do I think is going to answer me? There's no one here. The days pass in terror, the nights don't end.

I remember my mother, my father, my brothers. All of them. I cannot fathom why Jaanbaz's brothers have imprisoned me. What is their objective? What do they want from me? Does no one in this country have the slightest compassion? Every single day, I requested Jaanbaz's uncles to send me to my husband in India or to get Jaanbaz to come here, but they paid no attention. None of them felt

The Taliban and I

any sympathy or kindness. On the contrary, they said, 'Isn't this your country? The place where you lived once is in the past. *This* is your home now.'

My home? Is this my home? But how can I live in this land, in this house? How can a country where civilisation has not entered, where people have no such thing as a heart, be mine? And then there's the lack of food. This country has a severe scarcity of food, and whatever little there is does not make its way into this house. Not for lack of money, but because of rules. Sadgi and Sultanbibi have the right to eat all they want, because their husbands steal food for them. I am astonished at their behaviour. I belong to the civilised world, I cannot imagine stealing food. One day they are caught and punished.

It is a day of fasting, and I am fasting with everyone else. No food will be prepared, what will I eat anyway? I have no wish to cook just for myself. It's almost evening, and I am trying to decipher the Koran in the veranda. What does it actually say? Why do Muslims cite it to justify their actions? Jaanbaz bought me this Koran in Calcutta; all the verses have been translated into Bangla. I am trying to make sense of them.

My sister-in-law's son Dur Mohammad arrives. His mother Samala died of septicaemia when the placenta did not emerge after she gave birth to a child. He comes up to me with a packet and says, 'Where's Sultanbibi, Saheb Kamal?'

I answer in Pushtu, 'Why, what's the matter?'

'Musa has sent eggs and sweets for her.'

'Leave them with me,' I tell Dur Mohammad.

'No, he has said I must give them to her.'

'Doesn't matter,' I tell him firmly, 'leave them here.'

The poor fellow hands me the eggs and sweets and runs off. I give some of the sweets to Gulguti—she loves them.

Suddenly it occurs to me that the Koran is lying open in front of me. It may not be my religion, but it's a religious symbol nevertheless, and all religious symbols are sacred. Did I just steal those sweets with the Koran as my witness? Is this how low I've sunk in the past four years? I return the sweets and eggs to the packet and give them to Sultanbibi. Still, I feel small, as far as my conscience is concerned. Am I the same Sumi who was punished in her childhood by being made to kneel down for half an hour with bricks on her shoulders?

How old was I then? Barely eight or nine? I had a cousin whose nickname was Kelo, short for Kalidas Mukherjee. We were about the same age, he was only a year older than me. The grown-ups at home never bought us anything to eat from shops or restaurants. Everything we ate was homemade.

One day my father told Kelo and me, 'Come to the market with me. I will do the shopping, and you will bring it home.'

We went with him to the market with shopping bags. His first stop was at the grocer's, where he bought three litres of mustard oil in a large can and two kilos of sugar, and handed them to us to take home. There was a small sweet shop on the way from Baguiati Market to VIP Road on the right-hand side. It has become quite a big shop now. Kelo and I saw they were frying sweet, juicy jilipi there. Our mouths were watering; we stared greedily at the sweets. But we had no money. I immediately hatched an evil plan, the kind that tended to sprout in my head but no one else's. Telling Kelo to wait, I walked up to the shop. Then, as soon as the shopkeeper there turned his head away from the stall, I grabbed a handful of jilipi and ran. That was when the accident occurred, and the can of mustard oil slipped from my hand. When my father found out, he made me kneel down at home as a punishment. Mind you, my grandmother sat nearby, fanning my legs to prevent mosquitoes from settling on them. Not that this relieved her of all her responsibilities. 'Can't you scratch my legs, you stupid hag? They're itching. Just you wait till I get free,' I screamed.

And now, in my mature years, I have forgotten the lessons my father taught me. How unhappy he will be to hear of my downfall.

Women in Afghanistan don't have too many demands. A room of their own, a carpet, a large tin trunk and some clothes are all it takes to keep them happy, as though it is a windfall. Not that there's anything more to get here. And in case a woman owns something more than this, how proud she is of it. Crystal plates and glasses, perhaps a lantern, a sewing machine, or steel utensils. And, if at all possible, a husband who's hers alone. This is enough to make her the happiest woman in the world.

How hard the women here try to be fresh and fragrant for their husbands. No matter how grimy they are all day, as soon as the sun dips in the west and the last of the vermilion-streaked sunbeams says goodbye, all the wives will go into their rooms, wash up, change into nice clothes and wait eagerly to be informed of their husbands' return. There's no exception to this rule.

The sight often makes me want to copy them. If only Jaanbaz were here, I tell myself, I would also dress up for him. The very next moment, I berate myself. This is shameful. Why should I spruce up for a man for whom my love is dwindling bit by bit each day? I am who I am, my flaws are part of me. Why do I have to offer up my body afresh every time? He knows every bit of me already—dressing up for him is farcical.

Besides, do I really have a husband? Or a love to call my own? Or am I cursed like one of those mythical characters?

Neither the mind nor the heart brooks any obstacles. A heart that sweeps aside all barriers wants someone; it seeks to be thrilled by a loving touch. But I simply cannot conjure up Jaanbaz's image for this. Every time I do, it's anger and disgust that replace love. I cannot, I simply cannot make room for him in my heart any longer. I give up and admit defeat.

To give my exhausted mind some rest, I set off for my sister-in-law Guncha's house. Walking is the only way to get to Alekdar, where she lives.

Guncha's house is about an hour and a half on foot from Sarana. I leave early in the morning with my adopted daughter Tinni.

I quite enjoy spending a few days in Guncha's house when I visit her. My chamber usually remains closed during this period. Guncha has two daughters, Zorgol and Bilkis, and a son who was born between them, Akbar. Her second husband, Asam Khan, is a decent man with a sense of humour. But he has cheated Guncha. Neither he nor his first wife showed any compassion to her because she is Asam Khan's dead brother's wife. They spent lakhs on their own daughter's wedding but packed Guncha's girls off with nothing but their clothes.

Leaving Rastul Khel behind, I walk along Ambar Khel. Suddenly a jeep stops in front of me. I stop too. Four or five men get out, and one of them asks me in Pushtu, 'Where are you going, woman?'

I realise they're the Taliban. Gathering courage, I say, 'I'm going to visit my sister-in-law.'

'Why are you alone?'

'My husband is in India. Who will come with me?'

'No one else at home?'

'Even if there is, they don't accompany me.'

'Then why are you out alone?'

Their line of questioning infuriates me. I say, 'Very well, if you don't like my going out alone, all of you can come with me.'

One of the Taliban soldiers says, 'You still wear Punjabi clothes? Why don't you obey the fatwa?'

'Because I see no need to.'

'How dare you argue with us? Do you know who we are?'

'Why wouldn't I? You're the Taliban.'

They argue some more and then leave. I continue walking. My sole objective is to become familiar with these streets.

It's afternoon by the time I arrive at Guncha's house. Here I learn that the conflict between Gulbuddin Hekmatyar's Hezb-e-Islami and the Taliban is escalating. Thousands of Taliban soldiers have begun arriving. Modern rockets, grenades and missiles are being supplied to them by Pakistan. Many Afghans are also joining the Taliban, though others are fighting against them on the side of the Hezb-e-Islami.

The war is confined to the area between Gardez and Charasiab. Kabul is just twenty minutes away from Charasiab. Battles are raging everywhere, and we are caught between the war and the oppression of the Taliban, who assault us, rob our homes, and then blame Gulbuddin, leader of the mujahidin.

Terror has returned to Afghan homes. Everyone here is aware of the war. The smell of gunpowder hangs in the air. It's difficult to breathe. The sound of cannons is deafening. Rivers of blood are beginning to flow from thousands upon thousands of the dead. Once again, corpses pile up in ditches. Those who came back home from Pakistan under the impression that peace has been restored are considering fleeing again. I hope the war gets worse because then it will force everyone to go to Pakistan. And I will go with them.

Unfortunately for me, the war stops. And I remain where I am. The hands of the clock have stopped at midnight.

10

The year is 1969. The only word you hear all around is 'Naxal'. There's just the one slogan, 'Long live the revolution', just the one assertion, 'China's chairman is our chairman'. I don't understand what these things mean; I'm not old enough. But Tyaton comes over sometimes to explain everything. It isn't as though he's much older than me, but he has grown up overnight—he has changed. Bachchu, Tutun and I sit with him to listen to his Naxal exploits.

Many of the fine boys in the neighbourhood have joined the Naxal party, the CPI(ML). They gather in the field next to our house as soon as darkness falls. No one else knows what they talk about. I asked Tyaton one day, 'What do you people discuss?'

Putting his fingers on his lips, Tyaton says, 'Shhh, don't tell anyone. We discuss how to begin our action.'

Then a Central Reserve Police Force camp comes up nearby. The roads echo with the sound of the policemen's boots.

The CRPF is supposed to capture Naxals. Since our Tyaton is young and inexperienced, so he's the first one they catch. I feel very bad for him. Poor Tyaton. His mother is dead, and his father lives elsewhere. He's growing up in the care of his uncle and aunt. But I know the secrets of his heart. 'You're my closest friend, Sumi,' he says, 'I can tell you everything.'

He has shared with me his sorrows and sufferings. Tyaton sings beautifully, with a wonderful sense of melody. He sings popular Bengali and Hindi songs, as well as revolutionary ones from his ideology. All of us are charmed by his full-throated singing.

But all of this is within a limited timeframe, for I have to go back to school, studies, music and dance lessons, and, of course, constant mischief. Not all of it is fun, but I have to do it anyway. There's another task alongside my other activities, which is to conduct dolls' weddings. There's a new wedding every week. Khachu's son—her formal name is Manju—is getting married to my daughter. My grandmother is the cook for the feast, and my uncle will do the shopping. My family holds a grand banquet for the wedding, but there's no feast from the groom's side. I'm furious at this. I've seen the lavish arrangements the in-laws make to celebrate a bride's arrival at her husband's house. Then why not for my daughter?

Suddenly I discover that Khachu is an evil mother-in-law. There's no other reason for the lack of a feast. Just you wait, Khachu, the next wedding will be between your daughter and my son. I won't host a feast either when I become your daughter's mother-in-law. I will torment her; I'll make her starve. No, I can't do that. I'll torment her, but I'll let her eat. After much thought, I go to Khachu's house, which is two blocks away from ours in the staff quarters' colony. Bakul is with me. She's catching fish with a thin cloth in the stream flowing over the sand and pebbles beneath the bridge.

Khachu says, 'Oh, if it isn't Beyaan. How are you? When did you arrive? Do join me.'

She has heard her aunt speak like this when addressing her daughter's mother-in-law. But I don't know how to respond, so I can only nod. Khachu says, 'You're an idiot, don't you know how to reply?'

Instead of responding to this, I say, 'Listen, Khachu.' I don't address her as Beyaan or anything, I feel shy. I tell her, 'Now my son will marry your daughter. Are all your children boys? You do have girls, too, right?'

'No, they're all boys, no girls.'

'How's that possible? My grandmother has daughters as well as sons. My mother has sons, and I'm her daughter. Look at everyone—your mother, too, has both sons and daughters.

'So what if they have daughters? I don't.'

'No, that's impossible. Didn't you see how Joga Kaku had a son, and then he brought a daughter home from the hospital? You do it too.'

'All right, I will. But she can't be married yet, she has to grow up first.'

'Then return my daughter to me. Return all the clothes and jewellery and shoes too. Everything.'

Khachu doesn't agree to this proposal. How can she? My daughter is her daughter-in-law, after all. I insist. When she keeps refusing, I give her a shove. Unable to maintain her balance, she tumbles into the stream and hits the back of her head on a pebble. It starts bleeding. I run home and hide behind the water tank on the roof. I know they will be coming soon to complain to my grandfather. I'm not worried about my grandmother or uncle; it's my grandfather whom I fear. It's excruciating when he hooks the curved handle of his walking stick around my neck and tugs at it. My uncle cannot beat me up; all he does is tie my hands behind my back, though he unties them soon afterwards. 'It's hurting her,' he says, 'look how the blood has gathered under her skin.' But my grandfather gives me a sound thrashing. He cheats me too; he lies to me and goes off for plays and recitations of the Ramayana without taking me along. I lie to him, too, to teach him a lesson—instead of going to dance classes, I meet the policemen whom I refer to as 'Uncle' near Gate No. 3 and listen to them swapping ghost stories. I climb the guava trees for their fruit, I climb the mango trees and eat the raw mango with salt. Three weeks later, the dance school sends word that I haven't been going for classes. My uncle says, 'Why don't you go to dance class? Do you have an explanation?'

After some thought, I say, 'Yes, I do.'

He says, 'Very well, what is it?'

'Everyone else wears double ghungroos. Mine are single. That's why.'

'Oh, so that's why you don't go. Did you hear that, Baba? I was wondering why she hasn't been going.'

After this, the inevitable happens. I get not one pair but two pairs of double ghungroos. Now I have no choice but to go.

These days, I sometimes think about the lies I told, which my uncle believed, without checking for their veracity. It must be the truth since I was saying it. My lie was pure truth for him. I lost to my conscience, but he didn't.

All these years later, defeat and despair keep chasing me. I have a home, I am a homemaker, but there are no children in my home, no one whose lies I could blindly accept to be true. It's an agony I am never going to be relieved of. I am tempted to fulfil my desire to be a mother to children, but the hatred and aversion for me here and the Taliban's fatwa have throttled my desire. My child will be acknowledged as an Afghan child, on whom I will have no claim—it will be its father's alone. Still, the loneliness of my hours of leisure drives me mad.

11

I haven't been able to spend a single day in peace after my return from Afghanistan. All sorts of crises bear down on me and consume me.

No, it isn't as though my parents or anyone else in the family has rejected me. I don't know how welcome I am, but they have surely not forsaken me. Still, my mind is not at peace, I find no calm anywhere. Those who were once my closest friends in Kolkata now avoid me for marrying a Muslim from a foreign country. Apparently, I can no longer lay claim to my religion. I am embarrassed to think that I once belonged to a civilised society; I am ashamed to acknowledge that I live here amongst neighbours and leaders of society who claim to be secular.

I abhor these people who say one thing and do another. How much can the educated, refined Hindu Bengalis of our country be trusted? Can you trust them to honour their wives? I know many men who treat their wives like maids and even kill them or force them into prostitution when they are finished with them. Most men believe that a woman is born to play the roles of maid and whore, whether she's their wife or a woman they meet on the street. A woman who tries to transgress the bounds of these roles must be fed to the dogs. If women go out to work or are late getting back home, their husbands or fathers or brothers become suspicious and interrogate them, and neighbours look askance at them. But women are not so narrow-minded when it comes to men. And who's listening even if they are? Are women even human? Imagine listening to their views! Injustice, oppression, neglect and a lack of rights are all that's reserved for women.

I want to breathe freely, I want to stand beneath an open sky, I want to go far away from these selfish people.

I'm standing on the shore. The sea stretches out in front of me. I haven't been able to leave behind selfish people permanently, but I am in Digha in order to forget them for some time. I love the sea. I think it has its own language. There's no selfishness about it. I went to the seaside with my grandparents in childhood but did not understand what the sea was saying; I did not engage with it in the same way. Or perhaps there was no urge to understand it then.

Possibly I wasn't ready for it. I lacked the necessary depth, for I was a mere adolescent at the time, the age at which children are slapped by their parents for being naughty. I used to rip up my mother's and grandmother's saris to make clothes for my dolls. I had no idea then that when I grew up, I would rise in protest, that I would declare war on injustice, even pick up an AK-47. But reality has made me what I am today, a reality that no one can deny.

Sitting by the sea, I am flooded with memories. My thoughts compete with the rise and fall of the blue waves in front of me. An enormous wave is coming towards me, fierce and unforgiving. It will sweep everything away. Towards what?

This is how my emotions swept me away once on the waves of Sourav's charm. There was a scent of Sourav everywhere; the very air was permeated by Sourav. The world revolved around Sourav, not the other way round. I needed Sourav for music, for banter, even for fights. Sourav was everything to me. And yet one day, he was no longer around to share these with. He was lost to me. All that remained was remorse and regret. Everything seemed to have come to a stop. I was only twenty—just when it was time to decipher the mysteries of life, I discovered instead the hurtful stigma of being young and desirable. Those very mysteries turned into the menacing shadows cast by my coming of age. I was repulsed by the thought of lifting the veil on them. Can desire be so naked?

I had ended things with Sourav at Ronita's house that day. His appeal was a thing of the past for me, but the abrupt end to our relationship made me restless every moment—a fire raged within me all the time. I tried to wipe out his existence like a bad dream but could not. Sourav had tarnished the idea of intimacy for me by sleeping with Ronita.

I met Jaanbaz two years after this. He was pleasant, sensitive, natural. In no hurry to sleep with me. He felt no need to do anything extra to express his feelings. The love that should not have been, could not have been, came to be. I could not turn him down. I used to question myself often: Love with a Kabuliwallah? Is it even possible? It was. Jaanbaz's personality made it possible.

But it would be a mistake to assume that every man in his country is a gentle lover like him. The opposite is true. Most Afghan men consider women nothing more than companions in bed. There is no intention or obligation to give as much as they receive; the women are supposed to keep satisfying the men. Their own pleasures lose their way in the dark maze of Afghan society. It's the same for many women in my own country and elsewhere as well. Not only are men incapable of giving, even the way they receive is ungracious. And women only give all their lives—how much are they allowed to receive for themselves? A woman has to accept all kinds of difficulties just so she can love a man. Accept and live, or live because you must. Women have to live because they must. In the West, their likes and dislikes amount to something. Even in a country like India, which is still backward in many places, they do to some extent. But not in Afghanistan. Here, women are sold for money. Any Afghan man with some money can buy a wife of his choice. Dark or fair, short or tall, young or old, virginal or a widowed mother of five—it's all a matter of his choice. A woman is nothing but a commodity on sale, waiting for a customer.

A gust of cold air hits me. I wrap my sari tighter around myself. It is evening. I have been sitting here since late afternoon. Shibani and Meena were gathering seashells earlier. Now they are sitting beside me, singing. While thinking about Afghanistan, I had nearly forgotten about them.

Meena lives with me. I met her for the first time after I returned to Kolkata from Afghanistan. She has been a witness to many of my ups and downs. And Shibani is my friend, too, though not from my childhood. She's Jaanbaz's friend's wife. We met in December 1995. I never met her husband, for he died of a heart attack four months before my return. He was only forty-two. A lonely Shibani found a friend in me. Her life after her husband's death was no exception to what invariably happens in such cases. She has to manage her daughter and the household single-handedly. Memories of her husband haunt her. Overcome by emotion, she tells me sometimes, 'You know, he used to say he'd go crazy if I wasn't standing at the door when he came home after work.' She begins to cry as she says this.

It's getting late. The seaside is almost deserted now. We rise to our feet and begin walking towards our hotel. A few stragglers can still be spotted. Our bodies, sticky with the salt in the wind, are cooled by the sea breeze. We turn right towards Hotel Sea Hawk. The rooms have views of the sea.

I don't know what time it is. Meena is fast asleep next to me, with Shibani beside her. I cannot sleep, my thoughts won't release me—they grab me by the throat given half a chance.

I constantly keep thinking of Tinni. I can't help that. It's been months since I last saw her or held her close. I had so many dreams for her—that she would go to school, learn music, be accomplished. Those Afghans would see for themselves then that plants can grow in the desert too; they can sprout beautiful flowers and fruits. I did not succeed; I was defeated. I cannot free myself of the despair from this defeat. I know what Tinni's future might be like. Perhaps she will be sold for a paltry sum and forced to spend her life as a maid for an old man under the guise of his wife. Or else she will join a young man in bed and be his wife, only to accept his next marriage a couple of years later.

Kharot lives next to Jaanbaz's family. His mother's name is Gulguncha. I call her Chachi. Her husband's name is Rahmat Khan. They have four sons and four daughters. The eldest daughter Sasuka is married into a family now living in Karachi. They left for Pakistan in 1980 at the first declaration of war. An affluent family, they run a shop there.

Sasuka's husband's name is Sultan Mohammed. His father Akhtar Mohammed has been on the Haj four times and is a Haji. And yet, in 1992, we heard that he used to make fake passports to send Afghans and Pakistanis to India. He had his people posted at airports to clear passengers with fake passports that bore Akhtar Mohammed's code number. Many from our village Sarana had arrived in Mumbai on Akhtar Mohammed's fake passports, discarded them in the streets, and turned into Indians. Akhtar Mohammed even had his people stationed in the Mumbai airport. His son Sultan runs the racket now.

Akhtar Mohammed's eldest daughter Zoro is married to her sister-in-law Sasuka's elder brother Kharot. Gulguncha's other daughters are named Basu and Ameena. Basu is married to Kala Khan of Charda village. After his mother died in 1994, Kala Khan's elderly father was all alone. Since no one can live that way, a hunt began for a bride. Finding a bride for a seventy-year-old man is not an easy matter normally, but in Afghanistan it's surprisingly simple—all it requires is money. And so, Kala Khan found a new 'mother' for himself, paying the equivalent of three hundred and fifty thousand Indian rupees for Shamsulla's fourteen-year-old daughter. According to tradition, the old man would go to his new bride's house before the wedding and spend the night in a room with her. Kala Khan was very busy; he had to get his father dressed up, take him on his motorcycle to the bride's home and then go back early the next morning to fetch him. I was at Shamsullah's house to examine a woman who was about to give birth. The old man's child bride was seated there. Her aunt told me, 'This girl is going to be your neighbour Basu's mother-in-law.'

Was I supposed to stand by and watch this abomination? I could not. I blurted out, 'Aren't her parents here?'

The girl's aunt answered, 'Why shouldn't they be? That's her mother sitting there.'

So I asked her mother, 'Instead of giving her in marriage to an old coot, why didn't you drown her?'

The mother began to cry for the benefit of onlookers. Smiting her forehead, she said, 'We're very poor. If we eat one day, we have to starve the next. I sold her for a lot of money.'

I had nothing to say after this. I gazed at the girl. An unknowable grief was evident in her expression. Her body radiated exhaustion. At fourteen, her life was over before it could begin. She may have had a lot of dreams, many hopes and expectations. But a monster named poverty had taken it all away from her. She had throttled her own desires to mitigate her parents' poverty. She didn't complain, didn't protest—she showed no sign of resistance. It was beyond her abilities. And even if she were to protest, who would listen to her? Women are not supposed to resist; they are nothing but sacrificial lambs. Just chant the incantation and chop their necks off.

But why?

Are they born only to suffer? Surely pleasure cannot be the monopoly of men—women have equal claim to it. If a seventy-year-old man can marry a fourteen-year-old girl and still enjoy the respect of society, why can't women get it too? If men don't hide their faces even after being proven guilty, why should women have to? Have all the shame and submission and discipline and burkhas of the world been invented only for women?

The entire night passes in painful rumination, without a wink of sleep. Getting out of bed very early in the morning, I find that my feet have guided me to the seashore. Like every other day, the sun is a huge hemisphere on the eastern horizon, popping out of the sea. The water reflects the tenderness of dawn. The waves haven't yet come up to the beach, the waterline is much further away at low tide. I walk eastwards, across the sand, with the sea to my right and the beach to my left. Which of the two attracts me more?

A little further on, I come across fishermen emptying their catch on the sand. I go closer. There's a large crowd around the piles of fish, and I merge into it. I notice a particular kind of fish with swollen bellies. Being inedible, they have been discarded by the fishermen.

The loveliness of the early morning is dissipating, the waves are getting more turbulent. The sunlight is glittering on the sand now. The tenderness of the morning vanishes in an instant. The harshness of the sun is tiring my body and mind, the breeze has lost its rhythm. The day is young, and the sunbeams are playing hide and seek amidst the tall tamarisk trees. I am walking back to the hotel.

As I enter the hotel compound through the back gate, my eyes are drawn to the left side of the garden. There's a swing, and a variety of flowering plants. The jasmines are blooming, and so are the tuberoses. The air is heavy with their fragrance. The area around the swing is still in the shade, and I feel a great urge to sit on the swing and fly up and down. I go up to it and sit down.

Suddenly someone calls from behind me, 'Sushmita, is that you?'

I turn around to find Tapashi standing there. An old friend, a classmate from Chittaranjan where I spent part of my childhood with my uncle's family. One of four sisters, she was a very good student. She got married to Nirmalya from the village of Katrasgarh near Dhanbad. I'd heard they'd had a daughter. I jump out of the swing on seeing her, and she, too, is overcome with excitement.

'Tapashi! When did you get here? How come?'

I throw a barrage of questions at her. She answers none of them at first, only stands, gripping my hands tightly with hers and looking intensely at me. Her eyes are shining with joy. She says, 'I never imagined I'd see you again, Sumi. When I heard about you, I ...'

Cutting her off, I say, 'Never mind me, tell me about you. Where's your husband? Your daughter?'

Tapashi says, 'You'll have to go to London if you want to meet my husband. My daughter? She's in Kolkata.'

'Then who are you here with?'

I realise it's a stupid question. I'm not here with my husband either. It isn't necessary to go everywhere with your husband. Tapashi says, 'I'm here with my boyfriend for a couple of days. To have a good time.'

I am stunned. What's this she's telling me? When she sees my frown, she says, 'Why don't you say something? Are we not allowed to be with anyone except our husbands? What's wrong with that?'

Taken back, I stammer, 'No ... I didn't say that.'

Tapashi says, 'I'm a flesh-and-blood human. Are only men entitled to have physical desires? And am I obligated to satisfy my urges with no one but my licensed husband? Why doesn't he follow the same rule then?'

Tapashi tells me many things, all of it revealing her resentment and sadness, the pain of losing something. Why have things turned out this way? What has she lost? And why? I was feeling carefree earlier, but now I feel weighed down again. She leaves, promising to come to my room in the afternoon. I go back to my room, where Shibani and Meena have bathed and had their breakfast.

'Where did you go?' Shibani says. 'We waited a long time before eating.'

I go into the bathroom without answering. I felt a sense of lightness earlier when the morning seemed beautiful. It would have lingered had I not met Tapashi so unexpectedly. With a fatigued mind, I stand under the shower. How strange it is that anyone I meet says they're unhappy. Is everyone unhappy, then? And yet just twenty years ago, they were all happy. Who has snatched all their happiness away and locked it behind bars, and where? Tapashi was full of ideals, a full-throated singer, an independent girl—the object of our collective envy. Is this the same Tapashi who cares nothing for principles anymore? If Nirmalya is in London, why isn't Tapashi with him?

There is no unhappiness in my own marriage since I returned to Calcutta and reunited with Jaanbaz. Jaanbaz is a genuinely good husband. All the wretchedness of the past has ended. I adjust to some things, Jaanbaz to others. I am finally in charge of my own household, which includes Meena, me, and Gobindo, who drives my car. Since I returned to Calcutta, Jaanbaz has merely been a nocturnal passenger on this ship; he returns home every night only to sleep.

Sometimes I wonder, what if Jaanbaz had been like so many other Afghans? What if he had stopped me from going where I pleased, what if he had tightened the reins of my freedom? But he wants to do none of these. Whatever I explain to him is the ultimate truth for him. Even if it's a blatant lie. Sometimes I wonder what kind of man he is—does he harbour no anger or resentment? I make up imaginary lovers to upset him. He says, 'I know you well, my mad girl. I know you won't cheat on me.'

I never do anything to disrespect his faith in me. He meets all my needs. I only have to say I want to go somewhere, and all the arrangements are made at once.

Despite all this, there's something missing. I feel a sense of failure. One day I tell Jaanbaz, 'A friend of mine has invited you to her place in Kalyani to have sweets.'

He says, 'You think I have nothing better to do than going all the way to Kalyani from Calcutta for sweets?'

It's not as if he doesn't travel. He's forever going here and there, but it's always with his friends. He can give me every pleasure in the world except time. He treats me like an empress; he will bring the entire market home, lay it out in the yard for my benefit and give me unlimited amounts of money—to shop, buy jewellery for myself, and have it remade. Buy and remake, buy and remake. The emperor may not be mine, but I have the freedom to buy and remake. What more can I ask for?

The shower will probably run dry now. I turn it off. Nearly an hour has passed since I entered the bathroom. Shibani is reading the newspaper. Meena is standing in the veranda, gazing at the sea. It's nearly eleven, I don't want breakfast at this hour. I order a cup of tea.

The September heat makes me perspire as soon as I'm out of the shower. The bright sun is searingly hot. The wind coming into the room feels like it has passed over boiling water. I am waiting anxiously for Tapashi. I have to find out everything about her. How did she draw the curtain on the ideals that mattered so much to her? Shibani has been observing me. She says, 'What's the matter, Sushmita? You look so anxious, what is it?'

Forcing a smile, I say, 'Why, nothing at all.'

Looking intently at me, she says, 'I don't believe you.'

'How did you know?' I ask in surprise.

'The face is the index of the mind,' she answers.

'You know, the girl I was talking to this morning …' I tell her as much as I know. Now we're waiting for Tapashi. It's 12.30. The bearer brings our lunch. I ask Shibani to serve. I woke up so early that my eyes are smarting now. The perspiration rolling off my body only makes me more tired. Overcome with fatigue, I stretch out on the bed.

I don't know how long I've been away in the land of sleep when the doorbell seems to ring. It rings again. I slowly return to my senses the way anaesthesia wears off after surgery. I hear the doorbell again. Then, some sounds. After that, a poem appears suddenly in a corner of my mind. I push it away to check whether it's really the doorbell. Yes, there it goes again. I open the door to find Tapashi standing outside. Closing the door behind her, I lead her to the sofa. The sun is going down in the west, shaky on its feet. Shibani shifts in her bed to face the other way. Tapashi picks up the jug of water on the table and drinks straight from it. 'When did you get here, Sumi?' she asks.

'Two days ago,' I reply. 'You?'

She says, 'Yesterday afternoon. I'll be here for three more days.'

I'm about to ask her a question after some hesitation when Tapashi says, 'Do you remember Debika, Sumi? And Neelkamal? And Ramnath, Shampa … remember Shampa?'

Looking blankly into the distance, she continues in a low voice, 'You know, I remember every single one of them. But none of them remembers me.'

Suddenly agitated, she continues, 'There's no need for anyone to remember me.' Lowering her voice again, she says, 'How will they, anyway? My life itself has become mysterious. You know what makes me really sad? That no one understands me. No one even tries.'

Tapashi is asking the questions and answering them herself. I gaze at her in surprise. Both of us fall silent. The fan is spinning overhead. The roar of the waves is a constant backdrop of sound.

To lighten the mood, I say, 'You remember how we were caught stealing pickle from Ramnath's house?'

'Of course I do. Your kaka's friend, Samaresh Kaka, tied your hands behind your back.'

Laughing, I continue, 'Yes, and then Ramnath fell from the roof.'

'And how strange, Sumi, he didn't have a scratch on him.'

I say, 'Tapashi, you remember how we used to drink palm juice in the afternoons?'

Tapashi replies cheerfully, 'And we would start dozing afterwards, couldn't stand straight—we saw stars.'

'And do you remember what happened after that? My grandfather came after us with his stick. We had no strength left in us to run ... he gave us the thrashing of our lives.'

'Sumi! When I really got drunk years later, why didn't anyone thrash me then? Why did the stick stop so early on in life?'

I am silent, I realise there's something Tapashi's trying to tell me. She wants to share her pain with me. And yet I'm hesitant to ask her. Let her say it on her own. Shibani is awake now, and Meena's in the bathroom. It's 5.30, but there's still bright sunshine outside. Youth is transient, it gets over in no time. But old age never seems to come to an end, wringing everything out of you before setting you off on the last journey. As soon as it begins, so does the waiting to meet that final moment.

Tapashi looks a little awkward now that Shibani has woken up. I introduce them to each other. Then I tell Tapashi, 'If you don't mind, Tapashi, will you let me ask you a few questions?'

'I know what you'll ask,' she says. 'But ...'

I know she's nervous because Shibani is in the room. I say, 'She's my friend. You can speak freely.'

Tapashi says, 'I couldn't do it, you know ... couldn't compromise with something so wrong. So I left Nirmalya and came away from London.'

'But what did Nirmalya do?'

'In what order should I tell you? About having fun with other women in front of me? Or raping me when drunk? About getting involved in the trafficking of women? Or cheating people by taking money from them, making false promises of getting them jobs and resident permits in the UK?'

Tapashi is foaming at the mouth. I am stunned beyond belief. Trafficking in women? Cheating people? My head is spinning. I cannot see Tapashi clearly—the light in the room seems to have gone out in an instant. No one is speaking. I don't know what to tell her. Is her beautiful childhood or adolescence the only thing that's real, then? Her energy, her exuberance, all of us singing together, playing badminton on winter evenings. How could such a lively girl have ended up this way? Breaking the silence in the room, I say, 'How long were you in London?'

Softly she answers, 'Three years. Long enough to let go of my existence. I saw my dreams dying in front of my eyes.'

'Dreams don't die, Tapashi.' To lighten the mood a bit, I say, 'Aren't you going to introduce me to your friend? What's his name?'

'Friend? Not really. A temporary companion, you might say. His name is Aniruddha Roy.'

'Are you and Nirmalya divorced?'

'Divorce? No, I'll never divorce him. I won't let another woman be his wife.'

'But you're doing something wrong too.'

'Wrong? You call this wrong? He had fun with one woman after another right in front of my eyes. Was that not wrong? He got me drunk and forced me to sleep with his friend. Was that not wrong? If he did no wrong, why should what I'm doing be wrong?'

I tell myself what Tapashi is saying is logical. Are women alone responsible for fidelity? Tapashi doesn't speak much after this. She only says before leaving, 'I have nothing more to lose, Sumi. I love new men in new forms every day. I use each one, and as soon as I'm done with him, I set a new trap for a new lover. I get a strange joy doing this. Do you know why? Never mind … what's the point of tempting the pious?'

I stare blankly at Tapashi. I have no words. Tapashi keeps talking. 'You know, Sumi, the devil rears its head inside me when the men fall into my love trap. A fire starts burning inside me, and I make sure they burn in it too.'

She continues, 'I've bought a flat in Ballygunge. My daughter and I live there. I have a wild time when she isn't home. I won't give you the address; you haven't freed yourself from ideals and society and such things yet. Bye Sumi, we'll meet again. The earth is round, we're bound to meet again somewhere.'

12

Whether it's in our country or in Afghanistan, women are constantly lost to us. Ruma Mitra. She is dead. There's no one by that name in Afghanistan. She's known as Sabina here. She is a senior police officer's daughter. She fell in love with Jumma Khan, and a storm of adversity descended on her. Everyone at home attacked her, but she did not give in. Why should she? She was in love, and love is blind. Or at least blind in one eye and deaf in both ears. So let everyone forsake her if they must, let there be an avalanche of catastrophes. At an auspicious moment—inauspicious on hindsight—Ruma got married to Jumma Khan. 'She's not my daughter,' her father declared, 'my daughter is dead.'

All of Chinsurah, her hometown in the Hooghly district, used to love Ruma once. Now, it refused even to offer her a roof over her head. An aunt of hers did help her a lot, though. Ruma and Jumma managed to find somewhere to stay outside Chinsurah. Ruma had two daughters in quick succession. Then it was time for Jumma Khan to go back home. Ruma took her husband's hand and went with him to Afghanistan, where she has been since then. Many Indian women haven't been able to escape the death trap named Afghanistan after entering it. I may be the only woman who has. Ruma Mitra aka Sabina is still there. I don't know whether she will ever find freedom. She lives in a house with her two daughters and a son, but it's not a family. Her father is dead, and her mother will soon die, too. She will depart from this world with the heartbreak of having lost her daughter.

I'm a bad woman in the eyes of my husband's family, for I have covered them in shame by leaving Afghanistan. I have no regrets about doing this to people like them. Women are no less powerful than men—more, in fact. As they say, if the elephant knew how powerful it is, it would destroy everything. Sometimes I wonder why Afghanistan turned out the way it did. The people there have nothing, yet they will not move to other countries. Ninety per cent of the people starve; still, they won't go elsewhere to work. Is this any way to live? No one cares to free those of us who came to Afghanistan holding our husbands' hands.

This doesn't mean that Pathans have no love in their hearts. Take Shiraz Khan, a distant cousin of my husband's, the only son of his parents, who had eight daughters before him and prayed incessantly for a boy. He was the apple of his parents' eyes. His father was illiterate but had no hesitation in sending him to school.

Shiraz grew up and, at twenty-two, fell in love with the beautiful Jahanara, who lived about a kilometre away. In contrast to Shiraz's rich father, her father was very poor. Shiraz bared his heart to his mother, who saw no reason to object. She wasted no time, informing her husband, who could not possibly go against his wife's and son's wishes. Delaying seemed pointless, so he spent a great deal of money and brought the bride home for his son—an angel.

Shiraz's life overflowed with happiness, a condition in which he reposed blind faith in his wife. But Jahanara wasn't happy, which was not unnatural, for she was in love with her cousin Salim. She was only twelve the first time she kissed Salim, and even seeing him made her body tremble with desire. Every time he touched her, she felt waves of pleasure. Still, she couldn't resist marrying Shiraz, for she had lived a life of deprivation since childhood. Shiraz was a millionaire. Physical pleasure isn't the only pleasure, after all. She came to an understanding with Salim. Why create trouble when he could secure both physical satisfaction and wealth? Every time Jahanara visited him, it was with money. She went back to Shiraz with her sexual desire satiated, and when he took his wife in his arms, he had no idea she wasn't his alone. Shiraz considered himself extremely lucky—to him, his wife was an angel incarnate.

Shiraz went to the family-owned shop with his father but couldn't concentrate on work. His heart constantly flew away to touch Jahanara, his intimate memories sending jolts of electricity through his body. He stared at the clock all day, willing the hands to move faster to six in the evening when all his waiting would end. When he returned home, he called loudly for his mother, assuming his wife would be delighted to hear his voice. His mother knew why he called for her; all she sought was his happiness. But she had no inkling that this happiness was hollow, that woodworms had been eating away at it.

The month of Ramzan was here, a time of fasting and abstinence. The next day was Shab-e-Qadr. Jahanara was supposed to go to her parents' house to spend Eid there. But Shiraz wasn't willing to let his wife go for such a long time. His mother was in a quandary. Since her son would insist on accompanying his wife, would that mean Shiraz wouldn't be home on Eid? Finally, she decided that Jahanara should go for no more than a day. But Jahanara wasn't happy about this. How could she not be with her parents on Eid, how could she not celebrate with her brothers and sisters?

She sat morosely in a corner of their bedroom. Shiraz didn't go to the shop after saying his prayers, choosing to stay back instead. In the afternoon, he went to the mosque and came home to find his wife still sitting there, her face resting on her knees. 'What's the matter, my heart,' he asked, 'why are you so sad? Tell me.'

Jahanara said, 'You people are so cruel. You won't let me go home. Don't you know how happy my parents will be to see me? I already get blamed for not meeting them now that I've married into a rich family. Now if on Eid too, I …'

'But why don't you go? Who's stopping you?' Not that Shiraz was pleased to have to say this.

Jahanara wasn't going to let go of the opportunity. At once she said, 'Then tell your mother not to stop me.'

It had been eight days since Jahanara had left for her parents' home. Shiraz hadn't been there at all, not even for a day. He had no peace of mind and even questioned his wife's love for him. Why hadn't she asked him to go with her? He went through the motions of going to the shop every day, hoping to see Jahanara when he came back home. He waited for her impatiently, but Jahanara was quite happy where she was. She met Salim every day. Still, she was forced to think of Shiraz. Her Shiraz, who, she knew, loved her. Who could throw himself on the floor to ensure her feet didn't touch a speck of dirt. How could she cheat him this way? … But her guilt went only as far as these thoughts.

It was a Friday in 1992. Shiraz felt he couldn't wait any longer; he simply had to visit his wife today. He would go whether he was invited or not. His life was bereft without Jahanara. It didn't matter if he had to bend a little to call her back home.

Meanwhile, Jahanara was thrilled, for there was no one at home today; everyone had gone to Karachi. Salim was getting married, and they were all invited to the bride's house. Only Jahanara's younger sister Jaanbibi and their old grandmother had stayed back. Salim had already told her to meet him in the room on the roof.

It was forty minutes past twelve when Jahanara's grandmother opened the front door to find Shiraz standing outside. Delighted, she embraced him and drew him into the house. Shiraz couldn't wait another moment to see Jahanara. 'Where's your granddaughter?' he said.

'She was here a minute ago,' said the old lady. 'Must have gone up to the roof. Wait, I'll send Jaanbibi to fetch her.'

'No need,' said Shiraz, 'I'll go and surprise her.'

'Why not? Yes, you go fetch her, and I'll make arrangements for your meal in the meantime. I'll catch a chicken. Can you slaughter it when you come back downstairs—the men aren't home.'

She took Jaanbibi with her to catch a chicken. Shiraz climbed the stairs quietly, his heart hammering in his chest. He knew his wife would be overcome with joy on seeing him—she would shower him with kisses.

Shiraz was outside the room on the roof now. It didn't have a door, only a curtain. Salim and Jahanara were meeting here today because they knew no one was home. On other days, they met in a storeroom next to Salim's room. Jahanara was confident no one would disturb them here today. No one considers the impossible, after all.

Shiraz parted the curtain carefully and at once felt as though someone had stabbed him with a knife. He felt his bile rise in revulsion. A fire began to rage in his head, which sought to burn the two naked bodies in front of him.

He charged in, picked Salim up bodily and hurled him from the second floor roof to the road below like a stone. Salim fell, screaming. Shiraz looked down to find that Salim's body lay on the street, completely smashed. In the grip of an inhuman frenzy, he dragged Jahanara downstairs by the hand, still naked, into her grandmother's presence. 'What should the fate of this adulterous woman be?' he roared.

Jahanara's grandmother was mute. Little Jaanbibi couldn't understand why her brother-in-law had brought her sister here naked. Did he have no shame? What was her sister doing naked on the roof anyway?

People had gathered outside by then around Salim's body. His skull was split into two. He lay on his stomach, one arm folded beneath it, the other extended upwards. He didn't have a stitch on.

'Bring a kameez,' Shiraz told his wife's grandmother. 'Quickly!'

Still in shock, the grandmother brought a kameez. Shiraz ordered Jahanara to put it on. She obeyed him. Then without wasting a moment, Shiraz dragged her into his car and turned the key in the ignition. The car raced along the congested streets. His wife sat next to him, her legs bare, her head uncovered. Sweat was rolling off Shiraz's body. He knew what he had to do now. He also knew what lay in store for him: he would be hanged for murder.

I was at my sister-in-law Guncha's house at that time. Jaanbaz had left me in Afghanistan and gone away by then. Although Shiraz's agony and mine had nothing in common, I was trying to find a similarity somewhere. Shiraz's wife had killed his faith in her. It wasn't a question of sex—that was a matter of a few moments. But she had dishonoured his love for her. I felt contrite. My pain seemed to merge with Shiraz's, but his heartless reaction affected me too.

There's a shaggy mulberry tree in the middle of the yard of Guncha's house. It was two in the afternoon, and I was lying on a cot beneath the tree. It was hot, but there was some shade too. Guncha's husband, Rammazan appeared to tell me that he had spoken to Jaanbaz from Barid's shop, where Jaanbaz had telephoned. Didn't my husband want to talk to me? He could have asked Rammazan to bring me to the shop.

I had tried to telephone Jaanbaz in Maniktala in Calcutta and failed. The number had changed. I wrote letters and gave them to Rammazan to post.

When I came back to Calcutta in 1995, the wife of one of Jaanbaz's friends told me that her husband, Adraman had given her my letter to read. Learning what I had written about her and Adraman, she had torn up the letter. So Rammazan had betrayed my confidence in him back in 1992; he had opened my letter to Jaanbaz and posted it to Adraman's address instead. I hadn't imagined he would do such a thing; I used to think he was not as evil as the other men.

How could anyone leave me imprisoned the way Jaanbaz had? How can people love someone but leave them behind? And yet Afghans don't allow the women in their families to marry far from home, lest they cannot meet them often, lest they get no information in case of sickness. And the same people tell me, Shoma and Kakoli and many others, 'What are you upset about? *This* is your home. Your parents' home is no longer your own.'

And what was happening in Shiraz's house? What happened to Jahanara?

Shiraz shoved his wife into her room. One look at his face and his mother knew what had happened or was going to happen. She had never been fond of Jahanara.

Shiraz told his mother, 'This is my order. She will not be allowed out of the room from now on. She has to be in there as long as she lives. Don't mistreat her. Give her every comfort in the world, but she will never have my love. She will have to weep for it. Like a beggar, she will have to pray to Allah for his forgiveness. Still, she won't get it.'

And just then, a police jeep arrived. Shiraz was arrested even as his mother beat her chest and shrieked. Jahanara remained sitting on her bed.

In court, Shiraz confessed to having thrown Salim off the roof and killing him. The judge sentenced him to death.

His father fainted. How was he to tell his wife that their son was to be hanged?

Everyone loved Shiraz; they wept for him. His life was over at twenty-eight. Lying in his cell, Shiraz wondered what wrong he had done in loving Jahanara.

As the day of the hanging approached, Jahanara was close to losing her mind. She had never imagined such an outcome. She would never forget Shiraz's love for her. Through his death, he had kindled in her love for him.

13

I wake up suddenly. It's barely six in the morning. Living in Afghanistan got me out of the habit of being an early riser. But there's a reason I'm up now; the car has to be sent to the garage at eight. My uncle has been calling me every third day to check whether I've sent the car for servicing.

It will be there all day. I'll let Gobindo, the driver, take care of the car there and go on to Maniktala. I read the papers quickly as I drink my tea and leave at twenty past seven. The car stops when the lights turn red at the Rashbehari crossroads. I'm gazing at the people outside, some in search of a living, some going to school or college, some to their offices. Everyone's rushing, probably with no idea when they will be able to stop. Wait, who's that? Looks like Tapashi. I jump out of the car and call her name out loud.

Tapashi turns and starts walking towards me. The signal has changed and the cars are beginning to move. Telling Gobindo to drive on ahead and wait, I run up to the pavement where Tapashi is waiting.

'Look at you! Weren't you supposed to get in touch after coming back from Digha? What happened?'

'Will you do all the talking or will you let me speak?'

'No need to say anything here on the road. Come with me, the car's waiting over there.'

'You haven't changed a bit, Sumi. Still a storm.'

'If I'd been different, you'd have had to visit me in an asylum.'

Both of us laugh. We've reached my car now. When we get in, Gobindo says, 'Where to, madam?'

'Will you come to my house?' I ask Tapashi. Before she can answer, I tell Gobindo to take us home. 'It's been so long,' I tell Tapashi.

'Were you dying to meet me?'

'Of course. But since I don't know your address ...'

'Oh stop it, Sumi, you're such a liar.'

'How do you mean?'

'Listen, Sumi, you know my elder sister quite well and you have her number too. So if you really wanted to ...'

I have nothing to say to this. It's true, I do have Enakshi's phone number. I am embarrassed. I sit in silence, gazing out of the window. The car goes past Dhakuria towards Jadavpur. Tapashi's the one who breaks the silence.

'Well, why are you quiet now? You know, Sumi, my boyfriend wants to meet you.'

We're home. I tell Gobindo to take the car to the garage for servicing.

The Taliban and I

Tapashi says, 'Your husband will come home in the afternoon, won't he? I'll meet him at last.'

'Oh, you want to meet my husband? Then you'll have to stay the night. But never mind my husband, tell me about yours. Does he write? Or not even that?'

'All that ended a long time ago. I'm not in touch either, I see no need for it. I'm fine as I am.'

After a pause she continues, 'You know, Sumi, I'd never imagined I'd actually be separated from him. I had come to terms with a lot of things, but ...'

'Never mind the but. I know exactly what you mean, you don't have to spell it out. Will you answer a question honestly, Tapashi?'

'I will if it's a question that can be answered.' Tapashi looks at me in anticipation.

'Is it just ... you know ... with your boyfriend?'

'You know, Sumi, there are many bonds in this world that lie beyond social ties, bonds we don't know about. A man might torment his wife, but he will not allow his lover to suffer. And that's where the lover wins—at least someone considers her worthy. Even if it's temporary.'

Tapashi stops. She has tears in her eyes. She's biting her lip to stop herself from crying. The fans whir overhead. Meena adds something to the pot in the kitchen and there's a sizzling sound. I can tell she's observing Tapashi. I don't know what to do. What should I say to Tapashi? She looks at me suddenly and says, 'You're a writer, Sumi, there's a truth you must write about. That building a bridge between a husband and a wife today needs no love. All it needs is a woman who is willing to please the men who can further her husband's career. The bridge will be built automatically, and also, there will be no financial insecurity.'

Tears stream down her face. Her large eyes turn red. Tapashi is sitting in front of me. The old Tapashi was cultured, beautiful, self-controlled. Where has she vanished? Her very existence is gone.

Tapashi departs, leaving a mass of sadness behind. I remember the old days. I often ate lunch at her place. Her mother was an excellent singer, and Tapashi had trained in music too. She used to get calls to sing at neighbourhood events.

At her wedding, everyone asked Tapashi to sing. Her husband's brother-in-law stared at her in unabashed admiration before telling the groom, 'A voice like this will leave you with no need to eat or drink.' I'd love to know what he has to say now. Never mind eating or drinking, what about valuing her? I'd like to meet her in-laws too, who had said, 'Don't think of it as going to someone else's house. You've spent all these years in one home; now another one is waiting for you. We will be honoured when you step inside our family home.'

I want to know if they're feeling honoured today. Shouldn't they have said, 'We pray that you quickly win over your husband's bosses!'

14

I may have left Afghanistan, but I cannot forget my life there. My mind takes me back there whenever I'm alone, or in my bed in the darkness of night. Not everyone there was bad. Many hated me for being a Hindu, but not all of them. It wasn't as though no one reached out with some amount of compassion. Or else it wouldn't have been very hard to shoot, poison or burn me to death. All the invitations that came for Jaanbaz's family used to be addressed to me, and whoever I visited seemed gratified. All of them said there was no greater Pashtunwali than me, someone who followed their code of doing one's duties and respecting elders.

The Afghans believe there are no greater Pashtunwalis in the world than themselves. This is true. Here, in India, many people hesitate even to offer a cup of tea to someone who's come to their house. Afghanistan lacks the polish of education, but it abounds in the sincerity of its people.

Afghans struggle to survive, and then they die because their illnesses go undiagnosed. Or even if they are diagnosed, they are left untreated. Tumours burst and TB becomes fatal since medicines are hard to come by. Ulcers are commonly misdiagnosed as stomach aches from ingesting too much milk and ghee. Uterine cancer stops periods, which the women assume means pregnancy. Even the oozing resulting from breast cancer is considered a sign of expecting a child. But when nine months pass without giving birth, they say a djinn is preventing it. Which then leads to making the rounds of mosques and ancestors' graves, until eventually the woman dies.

That's not all. Sometimes news comes of the death of someone who had travelled abroad from some illness or in an accident. That was how Aamir Khan died. He used to live about twenty houses down the road from my in-laws' home. He was Ghulam Chacha's son Tila Khan's brother-in-law. The first time I went to Pakistan with Jaanbaz Khan, it was Ghulam Chacha who said, 'If Jaanbaz's wife comes back to Afghanistan, I will give my wife to him. And if she doesn't, he will marry again and give his new wife to me.'

Tila Khan's sister had been married to Aamir Khan just eight months ago. He was going to leave for India now. Wiping away his tears, he went while his wife stayed behind.

It's the day of Shab-e-barat. You can eat anything you want; no justification is required. Fasting will add to your bank of piety. Abu has invited me to her house to have sewai.

The Taliban and I

Suddenly Adam's eldest son, Rabbani, arrives to tell us that everyone is crying in Aamir Khan's house; news has come of his death in India. Abu and I rush to his house.

The cold is intense today. Aamir Khan's wife Zarina and his two sisters were warming themselves at a fire in the winter kitchen when the news came.

Zarina's face is as red as the flames in the fire that is now dying down. Her eyes are still, her lips are parted slightly. She's silent, inert. Her head isn't covered despite the presence of the elders. Aamir Khan's weeping sisters are with their mother, who's beating her breast and lamenting for her only son, who has been her mainstay after her husband's death. The boy had a tough childhood. Their lives had begun to feel comfortable only three years ago.

'Why did I send him to India? How many more of our boys will they kill? First the father, now the son,' laments Aamir Khan's mother.

His wife Zarina is silent. All that can be heard is her hammering heart.

Aamir Khan used to live in the Colootola area of Calcutta. He left early that morning on his motorcycle, starting his day with breakfast at a restaurant, followed by a visit to a debtor to collect the interest payment. Suddenly a bus charged at him like a demon, pulverising him beneath its wheels. He has left behind his mother, and his newlywed bride, whose eyes still hold dreams of their future together, whose body still retains the memory of his touch. She lies alone in her bed, facing an uncertain tomorrow. Aamir has no brother, so that's ruled out. Aamir Khan's family had paid for Zarina, so having her marry someone else would be a waste of their investment. Will Aamir Khan's mother agree to suffer such a loss?

Afghan moneylenders lead very different lives in Kolkata. But they don't forget the struggles of their families even for a moment. Whenever the Afghans here eat a delicious meal, they are reminded of the lack of food at home. For all they know, their children are surviving on dry naans.

Afghans are a fearful lot, strangely afraid of everything except war. They won't leave their homes at night, making sure to get in before evening. Not even an emergency can drag them outside alone after dark; they must be accompanied by four or five others. The entire population seems subdued, joining the war only for the sake of survival. They know by now that as long as the country exists, so will war—oddly, it is their source of succour. Two naans twice a day is a big deal for them. There is a wave of happiness when a hen lays eggs, or when a cow gives birth to a calf. If the calf's a female, they're over the moon.

They will exchange fire over a portion of potatoes. My brothers-in-law are not exactly level-headed. They often act whimsically. Musa has only harmed the family instead of doing any good. His wife's home is in Mushkhel. Before his wife moved into our house after their wedding, he would visit her twice a week. Euphoric about these visits, Musa decided he needed a motorcycle to make the journey since walking was out of the question. So he sold off the cow that gave the most milk. Another cow was the centre of everyone's attention, for she was about to give birth. Anticipation was at its height, with even the neighbours asking when the calf would be born. Another question that's on their lips constantly is, 'Do your hens lay eggs?' Those without a cow and hens are considered the poorest of the poor.

I remember visiting Jaanbaz's aunt Hamida. They had ten cows tethered in their yard. I sat in the veranda, wishing we had at least five. It seems hard to imagine now that I'm back in Calcutta that this is the woman I had become when I lived with people who lavish great care and attention on the chicks from their hens in order to protect them from the talons of birds of prey. They count them every day before shooing them back indoors.

Just as they count their children. There are a total of eighteen children in Dranai Chacha's house, ten of his own and eight of Nadir Chacha's. Every evening one of them counts all eighteen as he ushers them indoors. Then Asam Chacha counts them again when they sit down for dinner. There's an uproar when the numbers don't tally. It's the same story in every family.

The men and women of Afghanistan continue to live in blind faith. They consider the maulvi Allah's representative;

they're even willing to consume his saliva to cure themselves of ailments.

The modesty and reserve of the women are infinite. In India, we can at least think about our own marriage, mention it, discuss it. The women of Afghan society leave the room in embarrassment whenever there's talk of marriage. Wives don't even look at their husbands in the presence of elders. Of course, there are a few with no reserve at all. Security is scant in the lives of Afghani women, none of them can be confident that their husbands will remain theirs forever. Many of them even resort to so-called black magic to ensure their husbands' fidelity. I saw Sadia's sister-in-law try such things. The outcome was disastrous—her husband actually died. Not that these things don't happen in Bengal too; the most embarrassing tricks and solutions are advertised in the newspapers there.

But this is how they live in Afghanistan. To say that compassion and kindness are conspicuous by their absence is to put it mildly. Only a handful of people showed me any kindness during my worst days. My husband's family was among those who did not. My brothers-in-law kept telling me that sending me to India would be very expensive for them.

I tried to explain to them that they wouldn't have to spend a penny; all I was asking for was their permission. I kept hoping against hope, counting the moments. I spent my time walking through knee-deep snow to cut wood, light a fire, and warm my room. What could one or two logs of wood do to dispel the bone-chilling cold? But I wasn't allowed more. My brothers-in-law and sisters-in-law would lie in wait to pounce on me at the first chance. I avoided having too many conversations with them.

Am I supposed to forgive my husband's brothers?

All the neighbours used to say they felt sorry for me, but intervening was beyond them, because Jaanbaz's brothers were known to be vengeful.

I did a great deal to nurse my husband's sister Guncha when she was close to death. When she recovered, her husband Rammazan told me, 'I will never be able to repay you, Saheb Kamal. I will lay down my life for you if you ever need me to.'

Later, much later, when I begged him, 'Rammazan bhai, save me, save me from them—have mercy on me,' he said, 'What can I do if your brothers-in-law won't let you go, and if your husband doesn't instruct his brothers to let you go?'

Looking at him tearfully, I said, 'You had promised to lay down your life for me, Rammazan bhai. I'm not asking for your life, only for a car that will help me escape. I will never reveal your role in this to anyone.'

'Impossible,' he told me, 'I could never do anything so wrong.'

Still, I went to Guncha's house many times and pestered Rammazan bhai, hoping he would change his mind.

Each time Rammazan bhai said, 'It is my duty to take you back home with your honour intact. How can I allow you to escape?' Later, Guncha said, 'A woman who runs away without thinking of her husband's standing deserves to be shot.'

I wonder whether I would have faced such persecution had Jaanbaz been with me. Would it still have been necessary for me to run away? Would the death sentence still have been issued against me?

15

I lie in bed, reminiscing. What else is there to do anyway? ... The expanse before me is arid, bare. As far as the eye can see, there's nothing but sadness. And a mirage in the desert. My man.

The wind blows. It has its own language. Which says he isn't here, you won't find him here—he's far, far away.

The sun is searing. I walk on ahead. My heart will not stay homebound today. It is 1994. I have spent five whole years here in Afghanistan. Even searching with a fine-tooth comb will not yield my Bengali self here. I don't even know where or how I lost it. Let it go, let it be swept away. All I want for my broken heart is freedom. The love story ended long ago.

With a hundred thoughts running through my head, I walk into Jayar Shah's garden. Jalil's mother married her brother-in-law, Jayar Shah's father, after her husband died. Many Afghan families have such marriages. Some men live with two or three wives at the same time, and some women have five or six husbands in succession. A man can marry again while his wife is alive, but a woman can remarry only if her husband dies.

There's another kind of marriage too. Take the case of Asam Chacha's eldest son, Dinyar Khan, who's in India these days. He's only fifteen, but his mother Nakshira was very keen to get him married. Apparently, Dinyar is quite grown up! One day I asked her, 'But how will you get him married, he's in India.'

She answered, 'So what? The wedding can be held when he comes home.'

An adamant Nakshira began to look for a girl. She was determined to get Dinyar married and, at the same time, demonstrate that her authority over the family was no less than that of her husband's first wife Pablu's. Pablu did not take Nakshira's views into consideration when getting her own daughter Fouji married. Moreover, Fouji's husband's family did not send clothes as gifts to Nakshira's daughter Kafui, even though Pablu gifted clothes to everyone in the groom's family.

So, Nakshira was going to exact her revenge now. She would tell Dinyar's bride's family not to send gifts to Pablu's daughter. This desire to avenge her humiliation kept her busy. In Afghanistan, they don't count children in terms of their father but of their mother. So Nakshira began her search across villages and finally found a suitable girl in Kotwal. However, she was at least five years older than Dinyar. Nakshira's argument was that the bride must be old enough to make the naan they ate. A small girl couldn't use the oven; she would fall into it. So mothers of boys preferred older girls for their sons.

And so, the fifteen-year-old Dinyar who lives away from home is getting married today. I'm invited too. The groom is still abroad, so the mother will complete the rituals on his behalf and bring the bride home. All this to take revenge on her husband's other wife, for which her son may well have to pay the price all his life. And Dinyar's own wife may end up sharing her husband's home and bed with another woman.

There's no escape, only a mirage. And yet it is this mirage of Jaanbaz that attracts me, that makes me laugh and makes me cry. In my imagination, he appears beside me, and my body responds. There's a tide in the river; it cannot recede. Spring is wasted and rain-filled nights are unbearable. Summer exhausts me, but there are no beads of perspiration. Still, he's there, and so am I. Not as we should be, but because we have to be.

There's a profusion of cucumbers and watermelons in Jayar Shah's garden. I pluck a couple of tender cucumbers. No one will take me to task for taking five instead of two if I want to. I have been here often to give saline to Jayar Shah's wife. Here everyone takes saline unnecessarily in summer. They also take saline when they get typhoid.

Jayar Shah's wife has a disorder; she eats earth. She can do without food, but she cannot do without soil. Apparently this is why she doesn't have children. It's not as though she's not strong enough to conceive. But she inevitably miscarries each time at five months. She was four months pregnant when she came to me.

She had begun to bleed. I didn't know what to do. I propped her legs higher than her body and gave her injections. Vitamin B Complex and progesterone. I told her family that she would need the Vitamin B injection every day and progesterone every other day. If this didn't work, she would have to be taken to Pakistan for treatment. But that proved unnecessary, and she gave birth to a healthy baby on schedule.

One day, when the boy was five months old, she put him in his cradle and went off to eat earth. Returning two hours later, she found him on his stomach. She picked him up and found that he had turned cold. She screamed. I was sent for, but it was too late. It was all over.

I turn back homewards with the cucumbers from Jayar Khan's garden. I stride ahead beneath the hot sun of the afternoon, thinking of Sita in Lanka. Like her, I too am imprisoned in a sense, though there's a great deal of difference. Sita did not think of liberating herself and leading the people, but that is foremost in my mind.

As I reach the front door of the house, I see a tractor approaching me. I pause. It comes up to me and stops. A man gets out and says, 'You're a doctor, aren't you?'

'I'm a fake doctor as far as the Afghans are concerned,' I tell him.

The man asks a woman to get out of the tractor. She comes up to me directly. I lead her towards my chamber. Inside, I ask her, 'What's the matter?'

She answers in fluent Bengali, 'My name is Shoma. Sugandha Mitra.'

I'm not surprised anymore. Shoma is about twenty-six or twenty-seven and has a beautiful, oval face.

'So you're walking on the same road,' I tell her. 'You must be here to seek freedom.'

'Are you angry because I've come to you?'

'Not angry, but I am pained. How many more women are going to pay the price for their mistakes? Are you also from Calcutta?'

'No, I'm from Purulia. My father works there. I have a sister.'

'What about your education?'

'Up to class ten.'

'And where did you meet your Mr Khan—was it in Purulia?'

Now Shoma gives me an account of how she met her future husband and eventually married him. 'I was just eighteen. The Khan family had a house in the town. Rashid Khan used to block my way when I walked to school and publicly declare his love for me. It went on for so long that eventually I gave in.'

'You married him immediately afterwards and came to Kabul?'

'No. My father found out and arranged for me to get married to someone else. But I ran away with Rashid on the day of the wedding. Rashid took me to a hotel in Jharia and then to another one in Darbhanga. Before that, he married me as per Islamic rituals, paying meher.'

'Did you convert to Islam?'

'Yes. The qazi made me recite the holy verses, and then they gave me beef to eat.'

'Weren't you unhappy about being made to eat beef?'

'I was. But ...'

'What do you want now?'

For some reason, rather than pitying her, I began to feel anger against her.

'My freedom. I know that nobody but you can make it possible. I have a daughter. She was born in Purulia. My parents used to call her Fuchu. I had a son here, but he's dead.'

'You want freedom? Why do I have to show you the way? You're an educated woman, you can use your agency to find a way to be free. The most I can do is give you some courage.'

Shoma's eyes fill with tears. But what am I to do? My heart weeps for her. Are we never going to get freedom, I ask myself. Must we stay away from those we love all our lives? Are we condemned to being nothing more than photographs for our families even though we're alive?

Shoma received news of her family in the first four years of her coming to Afghanistan. After that, nothing.

Could I have imagined the day I met Jaanbaz for the first time that he would be responsible for so many crises in my life? I recall the moment in which he had declared his love for me. It was a Wednesday in July 1986. Ruma had invited me home. I arrived at one in the afternoon to discover Jaanbaz seated on a sofa. It wasn't as though I disliked him. On the contrary, I liked him a little too much. The first reason for this was his formidable appearance and manly personality. He spoke very little and made no effort to be ingratiating.

'When did you arrive?' I asked him.

'A little while ago,' he said.

I sat down on the sofa opposite him. He was toying with his keys, his eyes on the floor. I felt like he had something on his mind.

'What are you thinking about, Jaanbaz?' I asked.

Ruma came in and said, 'I know what he's thinking about. Should I say it?'

'No, please,' Jaanbaz blurted out. 'Don't say anything. Give me some time, I'll tell her myself.'

Ruma said, 'All right, I won't say anything. But let Sumi eat first. Then the two of you can talk.'

It wasn't as though I couldn't tell what was going on. But I pretended not to understand and followed Ruma to the dining room. It was an unusual atmosphere. No one could refuse someone's love in such an ambience. I couldn't either when Jaanbaz said, 'Mita.' He was addressing me as Mita for the first time, though we had met at least a couple of months earlier. There was something in the way he called my name. I was transported by it.

'There's something I've been wanting to tell you for a long time.'

'Tell me what?'

'The truth, Mita, is that I've fallen in love with you.'

There was no pretence. Jaanbaz spoke freely and honestly. It was raining outside, but spring arrived in my heart, riding on the raindrops.

After this, we began to meet every day. Love blossomed —a strange kind of love. The kind of maddening love I hadn't wanted—a love that could only end in agony. I hadn't wanted this sort of love. I had wanted something where the bond remains even when love ends—a compelling relationship if not love, a togetherness if not an attraction between two bodies.

But what came about was the very love I didn't want. That too, from whom? Could such a love survive social pressure? I was like a leaf blowing in the wind.

He drew a response from my heart. I forgot everything else in the world. I waited impatiently to see him. But how was I to convey my pain to him? Who was this Jaanbaz, how long had I known him anyway, where had he come from, how much did he want me, was he mine alone? I asked God for strength and clarity.

I love Jaanbaz. I love him very much. My heart aches at the thought that he isn't with me. There was a time when I hurt myself in trying to hurt him. Anyone who could draw forth tears from me was surely not just another person, but someone very special. I had many male friends with whom I went out, spent time, ate lunches and dinners. All of them were attractive in some way or the other. But in my eyes, they were not special. No sparks flew. Why then was I drawn to someone who was only a fleeting visitor? Why did I begin to yearn for a man to unite with whom I would have to scale many high walls? And yet, not even in a moment of weakness would I let anyone else take his place. To make Jaanbaz my own, I would have to free myself of my traditions. There was a long way to go. ...

I've been on a little journey into my past while Shoma waited. It's strange to think of love as nothing but my past. Returning to the present, I ask Shoma, 'Has your Mr Khan ever promised to take you back to India?'

I know it's absurd. Whether it's in India or Afghanistan—who keeps promises? I am asking Shoma these questions because I know I can't do anything for her. She senses something in the way I'm speaking to her and leaves. I am relieved. Not because she has left, but because I haven't had to make false promises to her.

16

All speculation has ended today. Many disrespected him or hated him. Many didn't trust him because he's Muslim. This distrust, this dislike will remain with these people here in India, but Jaanbaz has left.

How can I say he's a bad person? How will I deny his love for me, the bond between our hearts, or my loneliness? When he left me in Afghanistan in 1990 and went back to India, I had no one there to call my own—only an emptiness. Today I am in my own country, surrounded by my own people. But how much of that void has been filled? On the contrary, memories wind themselves around me like a serpent. Everything of his is in this room—he alone is not. There's no symmetry between the desolation I felt when he left me behind in Afghanistan and the one I feel now when he has returned to Afghanistan, leaving me behind in Kolkata. And yet, he seems to be right next to me.

How can I call him en evil man? I cannot, despite all that has happened. I go to the station to see him off. It is four in the afternoon. I'm sitting in the car with the windows rolled up. Meena's sitting next to me. Gobindo is standing outside to keep an eye out for him. When he left at ten in the morning for Chandni Chowk, he told me to be at the station a little after four. Swarms of Afghans are coming towards us. I gaze at them, my heart trembling.

They won't force me to get on the train with them, will they? They have gathered not too far away from my car. The cars are parked on the left. Everyone's waiting for him on Platform No. 9. Their eyes are fixed on my car.

I sit unmoving. He's leaving today; I don't know when he'll be back. 'I will come back to your home if I remain alive,' he told me. My home? Why did he say that?

There's no more time to think. The Rajdhani Express arrives on the platform. A wave of Afghans is rolling towards me. And among them, in the middle, him. Recognisable even from a distance, even in a crowd of thousands. Six and a half feet tall. A broad chest, a stern face, milky white complexion. A dignified gaze. A shock of black hair. Handsome, beautiful. He's striding towards me like a hero.

The clock in my heart begins to race. Suddenly I remember a giant naan and the inevitable kettle of tea. And buttermilk.

All of them come up to my car. I lower the window. He gets into the front seat. Now tears begin to stream down his cheeks. The climax is upon us. The eyes of the Afghans standing outside are brimming with tears too.

Suddenly the clouds part in the sky. A dull sun peeps out. If only I could forget my life in Sarana from 1989 to 1995 and the murderous and criminal ways of the Taliban, I wouldn't dream of opposing this large crowd of Pathans. I would surrender myself before them, I wouldn't hesitate to follow their bidding. But now, I have no response to their touching words. What will I say?

Jaanbaz gets out of the car, still crying, and hands me a bundle of hundred-rupee notes.

I protest.

'Keep it,' he says, 'I won't be here now, who's going to give you money?'

It's true, he has left no stone unturned to ensure I have money. He knows my needs.

He tells me again and again before leaving, 'Don't fight with anyone, mad girl. You fight with everyone, you have nothing else to do besides fighting with others. Don't talk back if anyone says anything to you. I won't be here—who'll take care of you if you lose your head?'

To Gobindo and Meena, he says, 'Don't leave even if she throws you out. You'll have to endure everything until I return. You know how angry she can get. But still, she loves both of you.'

He's moving towards the train now. Everyone else is weeping.

Jaanbaz walks on ahead like a robot. Then he turns to look at me, wiping his eyes. I cannot bear it any more. My clothes are wet now with my tears. He cannot be a bad man. He cannot possibly want to kill me. All the other Afghans crowd around me. 'Don't cry, we're here. You don't have to worry. Just send for us if you need anything.'

They're crying as I am. Some of them are consoling me with their hands on my head. Others are holding my hands. I am bewildered. Are these the same people that I met in Afghanistan? All of them know what I think about their country, what I have written earlier about their people. They seem to have nothing in common with the residents of Afghanistan.

Bad people? How can I say they're bad?

I might have been wiped out by now. My dreams could have been shattered. But Jaanbaz had stood like a rock. No one has succeeded in going around him to curb my freedom.

Perhaps their honour and conscience will be victorious one day.

I return home, pale and in pain. The house feels empty and hollow. I'm trying to staunch my tears with all my strength.

No more doubt, just a stillness. The newly-constructed flats on the east are like towers wrapped in silence. The sound of scattered voices drifts in from a distance. All the lights in the compound are twinkling.

It's a deadened evening. The night sky is covered in stars. But they hold no appeal for me. I failed to offer him any sort of fulfilment.

He left me once because of his inability to fight his community. He left me again today. He offered weak explanations when asked. I was hurt, so I condemned him with my eyes, making no attempt to understand his compulsions. I wasn't going to deviate from my principles because of the Taliban.

Tagore has said it's a sin to lose faith in human beings. I am confident that humanity will triumph one day, and the combined strength of the men and women of Afghanistan will pave the way for a peaceful future.

Afghanistan: A Timeline

1978: President Mohammed Daoud Khan and his family are assassinated. PDPA leader Nur Muhammad Taraki takes over as president and prime minister of Afghanistan. Soviet military is deployed.

1979: Supporters of Deputy Prime Minister Hafizullah Amin murder Taraki. The Soviet army invades Afghanistan. Amin is assassinated.

1989: Soviet troops withdraw from Afghanistan.

1992: Afghanistan becomes an Islamic republic. Jamiat-e Islami leader Burhanuddin Rabbani becomes the president.

1994: The Taliban form a government in a remote village.

1996: Civil war begins, and lasts till 2001. The Taliban conquer Kabul, establish their rule, execute former president Mohammad Najibullah, and crack down on liberties for women.

2001: Bamiyan Buddha is destroyed on Mullah Omar's orders. After 9/11, the US president, George W. Bush, demands The Taliban hand over the al-Qaeda head, Osama bin Laden. The Taliban refuse. The US and UK bomb Afghanistan. Hamid Karzai is made the head of Afghan Interim Administration at the International Conference on Afghanistan in Germany.

2002: Hamid Karzai is appointed the president of the Afghan Transitional Administration in Kabul.

2004: Hamid Karzai is elected the president of Afghanistan. He stays in power till 2014.

2014: Ashraf Ghani succeeds Hamid Karzai as the president of Afghanistan.

2021: The US forces withdraw after twenty years. The Taliban storm Kabul. Ashraf Ghani flees. The Taliban take command of Afghanistan.

Sushmita Bandyopadhyay's Timeline

1988: Sushmita marries Jaanbaz Khan, an Afghan businessman living in Calcutta at the time.

1989: Goes to Afghanistan with Jaanbaz Khan. He returns to Calcutta some time later to continue his business. Sushmita stays back with his family in Afghanistan.

1994: Tries to flee Afghanistan via Pakistan, but is captured and held back.

1995: Makes a second attempt to escape, and is captured again and threatened with execution. Ultimately she manages to secure freedom and returns to Calcutta.

2013: Sushmita goes back to Afghanistan.

2013: Sushmita is killed, presumably by the Taliban, outside the home of her in-laws in the Paktika Province.

Post-script

This English translation is a shorter version of the Bengali original, the purpose of which is to keep the focus on the author's personal-political story.